LIKE A NEW SUN

SIX CONTEMPORARY
MEXICAN POETS WRITING IN
INDIGENOUS LANGUAGES

Phoneme Media
1551 Colorado Blvd., Suite 201
Los Angeles, California 90041

First edition, 2015

ISBN: 978-1-939419-26-2

Library of Congress Control Number: 2015939339

This book is distributed by Publishers Group West

Printed in the United States of America by McNaughton & Gunn

Cover art by Soid Pastrana
Designed by Scott Arany

Phoneme Media is a nonprofit publishing and film production house,
a fiscally sponsored project of Pen Center USA, dedicated to disseminating
and promoting literature in translation through books and film.

www.phonememedia.org

Curious books for curious people.

LIKE A NEW SUN

SIX CONTEMPORARY MEXICAN POETS WRITING IN INDIGENOUS LANGUAGES

Edited by David Shook and Víctor Terán
with Assistant Editor Claire Pershan

POETRY BY

Víctor Terán
Mikeas Sánchez
Juan Gregorio Regino
Briceida Cuevas Cob
Juan Hernández Ramírez
Enriqueta Lunez

TRANSLATED BY

Adam W. Coon, Jonathan Harrington,
Jerome Rothenberg, David Shook, Clare Sullivan,
Jacob Surpin, and Eliot Weinberger

PHONEME
MEDIA
Los Angeles

*Guicaa Sarah Maguire, gunaa nanaxhi ladxidó', gunaa biaani',
gunaa bioongo' ruyaana' guendanacha'hui' ne guendasicarú.*

*For Sarah Maguire, loving woman, torchbearer, primordial
tree that blossoms with goodness and beauty.*

—VT & DS

CONTENTS

BRICEIDA CUEVAS COB, *CONTINUED*

FOREWORD

The arrival of the Spaniards in Mexico has often been compared to the appearance of extraterrestrials (more exactly, extraterrestrials before the age of science fiction, before we began to imagine what they might be like). The bearded white men with their horses and guns corresponded to nothing in the Mexican worldview; and, most disastrously, the auto-immune systems of Mexican bodies had no experience with Spanish microbes. It has rarely been said, however, that this was also an encounter of mutually incomprehensible poetics. (If the conquistadors were largely illiterate soldiers, some of those who followed them, particularly a few of the priests, had both education and curiosity.)

Spain in the 16th century was writing traditional ballads and romances, and odes and elegies and eclogues inspired by the Latin. The sonnet, newly imported from Italy, was the rage. Mexico in the 16th century—to speak of only one of its poetries, the Aztec—had eleven sub-genres of lyric poetry that remain known to us: eagle songs, ocelot songs, spring songs, flower songs, war songs, divine songs, songs of orphanhood (also known as "philosophical reflections"), tickling songs , and songs of pleasure. The great religious Spanish poets of the period, Fray Luís de León and San

Juan de la Cruz (St. John of the Cross) were humans who wrote in praise of God. The great religious Aztec poetry—preserved in the *Cantares Mexicanos*—came as a gift directly from the gods to humankind. More astonishingly, it is believed that the poems were themselves a kind of god, venerated ancestors summoned to earth by the supplications of the poets.

The Aztec figurative system famously yoked two elements to form an unexpected third: cacao was "heart and blood," misery was "stone and wood," fame was "mist and smoke," pleasure "heat and wind." (This tradition of conjunctions, seen through the eyes of Surrealism, would be reinvigorated, four hundred years later, by Octavio Paz.) A person could be a feather, jade, a cypress, a flute, a gold necklace, a city. Fray Diego Durán, one of the first priests who was interested, unironically said that their poems are "so obscure that there is no one who really understands them—except themselves alone."

Spanish poetry "conquered" Mexican poetry in the centers of culture, with the unforeseen consequence that the greatest Spanish-language poet of the second half of the 17th century (and indeed for two hundred years after that) was a Mexican: Sor Juana Inés de la Cruz. But poetry composed in the scores of native Mexican languages carried on in the countryside, along with traditional customs, beliefs, and ways of making art. Most of this poetry was, of course, orally transmitted, and was unknown outside of its communities until anthropologists and others began transcribing and translating the poems in the twentieth century. It is a poetry without a literary history, in the sense that it arrives to us late in the story and we do not know how it evolved over the centuries—as though the earliest known English-language poet was William Carlos Williams. And it is a poetry without criticism, in that we rarely know its poetics or its standards—the details of its composition, or what its listeners considered to be good or bad.

In recent decades, there has been an extraordinary new development in Mexico's indigenous literatures. Bilingual writers, educated in Spanish and conversant in Western modernism, are choosing to write in their native languages. As these are contemporary writers, their poetry and fiction is disseminated orally not only in live performance but also on radio shows, and, for the first time in these histories, in books and language-specific magazines. Some of the poets in this book use their native language as a way of enriching the modernist lyric. Others use modernism to re-imagine traditional forms.

What is happening in Mexico is being mirrored in many other countries where indigenous languages survive. It is partially a matter of ethnic pride. In the globalizing world, there is a counter-current that is emphasizing the local, celebrating what is different in the face of the monoculture, adapting the old ways in an era of relentless novelty. But it is also a culmination of modernism itself, the rallying cry of which was Joyce's "Here Comes Everybody." Twentieth century painting and sculpture is inextricable from its discovery of new forms in African and Native American art, or the stories, poems, and myths of tribal cultures that permeate modern literature. (For some decades there was, in France, a very blurred line between the Surrealist and the anthropologist.) Yet this was, in the last century, all one-directional: the indigenous feeding the cosmopolitan West. We are now at a moment—still in its early stages—where inspiration is flowing the other way. As this book demonstrates, the poetry written in Spanish, English, and French is one part of a complex of ideas and perceptions that is invigorating new ways of writing in Mazatec, Zapotec, Zoque, and Nahuatl, which may in turn lead to something else, somewhere else.

Eliot Weinberger, New York

PREFACE

There is a very important movement of literary production in the first languages of Mexico, and this speaks to the notable vigor of these communities to survive despite the injustices they suffer and have suffered for more than five centuries. This tendency to write in indigenous languages will continue, with or without the support of the Mexican government. The first communities of Mexico have understood that the issue of survival and development does not depend on the government but on their own actions and determination.

The challenge to defend and preserve our first languages and cultures is crucial in my country. The neoliberal onslaught that seeks to impose, for market reasons, hegemonic languages and to eliminate minority ones, through formal education and mass media, obligates writers to act, and not just stand around with our arms crossed. It's not enough to write, we must also raise our voices and organize ourselves to avoid the homogenization and impoverishment of human beings in favor of capital.

To write in an indigenous language today is far more than a political statement: it is a heroic act of survival. Survival because writing strengthens and extends the future of a language. Heroic because it means pain and suffering before the indolence of many of its own speakers, who forget their responsibility to their mother tongue, due to their desperate struggle to earn their day's bread; because it means to endure the disregard of governments and institutions, which promote a double discourse, on the one hand passing "progressive" laws but on the other not allotting the resources that would enable such laws; because it means discrimination on the part of mass media organizations and national publishing houses; because it also means desperation and sadness at not being able to hold the fruits of one's labor in one's own hands, not being able to publish it and share it with the community.

The works being written in indigenous languages today aren't greater world literature's lesser siblings. Poets like Briceida Cuevas Cob, Mikeas Sánchez, and Juan Gregorio Regino, to name but a few, prove that the literature known as "indigenous" is as powerful, artistically speaking, as that produced by writers working in dominant languages.

Besides serving to immortalize life and events, and helping us to think about and feel our common world from new perspectives, literature also functions as a defender of language. That's the importance of writers working in indigenous languages—they save their language and culture from being impoverished and disappearing.

Víctor Terán, Juchitan, Oaxaca

INTRODUCTION

I **began translating Víctor Terán's poetry** in 2008, initially working from his own translations from Isthmus Zapotec to Spanish. We met soon thereafter, in the city of Oaxaca, a six-hour bus ride from Juchitán, the cradle of contemporary Zapotec literature. There, sitting on the edge of my disheveled bed to record Víctor's reading the poems, I heard them in their original sonic glory for the first time.

After publishing translations in a wide range of magazines, including *Poetry* and *World Literature Today*, we toured the UK with the Poetry Translation Centre in 2010. It was on that tour, after a reading at the Wordsworth Trust in the rural Lake District of Northern England, that the idea for this anthology was born. At each stop on our tour, Víctor's chapbooks had sold out. What surprised our audience, beyond the beauty of hearing for the first time a language so utterly unlike English, wielded to its full auditory potential by its finest practitioner, was how *contemporary* the poetry was.

In the gardens outside Wordsworth's home, I asked Víctor which other indigenous Mexican poets he would recommend. The three he immediately answered—Juan Gregorio, who writes in Mazatec, Briceida Cuevas Cob, who writes in Yucatec Maya, and Mikeas Sánchez, who writes in Zoque—are all featured in these pages. To those we have added Juan Hernández Ramírez, who writes in Eastern Huasteca Nahuatl, Enriqueta Lunez, who writes in Tsotsil, and, at my insistence, Víctor Terán's own poetry.

The poets within exemplify the two dominant lyric modes of contemporary Mexican poetry written in indigenous languages. The first is the contemporary pastoral romance lyric, masterfully displayed in Víctor Terán's poems of love and loss. The second incorporates significantly more traditional mythology, like Juan Hernández' book-length poem about corn, which even reflects traditional Nahuatl mathematics in its structure. Alongside established masters like Juan Gregorio Regino and Briceida Cuevas Cob, it is especially exciting to feature some of the most innovative emerging indigenous poets. The poetry of Mikeas Sánchez, who writes in Zoque, incorporates the widest range of foreign references that I've encountered in any indigenous Mexican poetry, ranging from Wolof immigrants in Barcelona and a Macy's in New York City to her grandmother's Zoque curses.

Like some 90% of the world's 7,000 languages, the indigenous languages of Mexico are threatened with displacement by the dominant regional languages—in this case, Spanish. Although the languages represented in this anthology are some of Mexico's most robust, it is essential for their survival that their speakers continue teaching the language to the next generations of speakers. The production of indigenous-language literature can be an important part of that process, as much for contributing to the library of available resources in the language as for keeping the tongue culturally relevant and evolving. In the Zapotec community, for instance, the example of established artists like my co-editor Víctor Terán and Soid Pastrana, the visual artist responsible for our cover, have inspired the youth to invent new genres of indigenous expression, like the Isthmus Zapotec rap group Juchirap and the recent Zapotec-language comic book adventures of Spiderman. The conversation about endangered languages—and why it's important that we preserve them—too seldom raises what I believe to be the most compelling arguments in their favor: each language's unique literature. As an enthusiastic reader of literature from around the world, I'm saddened by the vast quantity of literatures—especially oral traditions—that we will lose in the coming century, but I'm honored and excited to play a small role in sharing the vibrant but threatened literatures of the six indigenous Mexican languages here anthologized.

Mexico's indigenous languages have a strained relationship with Spanish, and the place of indigenous-language poetry in contemporary Mexican literature exemplifies the one-way influence of the dominant language. Most indigenous poets working today are forced to translate their own work into Spanish, often their second language, with the result that their Spanish-language renderings don't always shine with the contemporary brilliance of the originals. The poets working in indigenous languages also reflect a thorough cross-section of indigenous language speakers in contemporary Mexico. Enriqueta Lunez, for example, actively sought to learn her traditional language as a young adult, not having grown up speaking it. Juan Hernández Ramírez writes concurrently in Nahuatl and Spanish, just as he lives between both languages in his everyday life. Víctor Terán has spoken Isthmus Zapotec since he learned to talk, and began writing poetry when he was sent to a Spanish-language school in Mexico City and had no one to speak to in his native tongue.

Most translators into the English, including the majority of those whose work is showcased in this anthology, also translate using the Spanish as an intermediary, though the responsible translator must acknowledge her limitations and seek to remedy them through at least a cursory understanding of how the original language works and sounds. In the case of this anthology, the translators are fortunate to count the poets as collaborators and friends, which I believe has resulted in these translations being the most accurate available—the lyricism of the originals shines brightly through in English. Jonathan Harrington lives in the Yucatan, where he's able to readily consult native speakers of Briceida Cuevas Cob's Yucatec Maya. Clare Sullivan has worked with Enriqueta Lunez in person, at workshops in Oaxaca, and Adam W. Coon lived with a Nahuatl-speaking family in Guerrero to learn the language.

It's an honor to have co-edited this anthology, which perfectly showcases Phoneme Media's nonprofit mission to introduce international writers to new audiences in English. On our website the reader can find a rich offering of supplemental resources, including audio and video recordings from the Nahuatl, Zapotec, and Zoque, Spanish-language versions of many of the poems included in the anthology, and additional context by *Like a New Sun*'s excellent cast of translators. I encourage readers to take advantage of the opportunity to listen to the languages, to get a better sense of just how beautiful the poetry sounds in the original. To do so, visit *phonememedia.org/likeanewsun*.

I'm incredibly grateful to our six poets and seven translators. I'd like to thank Eliot Weinberger for his foreword and support of this project; Dr. Daniel Simon at *World Literature Today*, which has championed indigenous Mexican literature more than any other publication I know; this anthology's assistant editor Claire Pershan for her enthusiastic embrace of occasionally treacherous tasks like transcribing the original-language poems; and tireless designer Scott Arany, who has mastered the typesetting of the glottal stop and nasalized vowel. Most of all, I'd like to thank you, reader, for your support. Welcome to the vibrant Mexico experienced by its indigenous-language poets.

David Shook, Los Angeles
Founding Editor, Phoneme Media

INDIGENOUS LANGUAGES

MEXICO

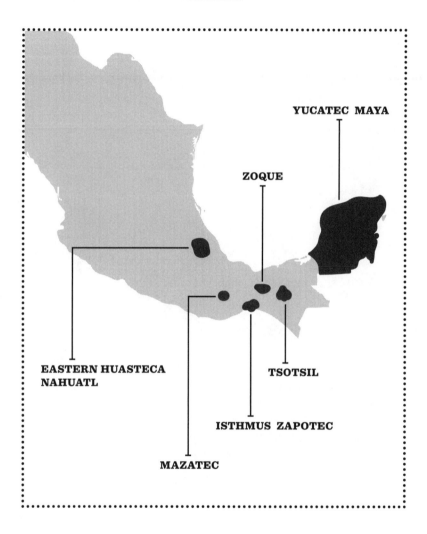

YUCATEC MAYA

ZOQUE

EASTERN HUASTECA
NAHUATL

TSOTSIL

ISTHMUS ZAPOTEC

MAZATEC

MAZATEC

OAXACA • MEXICO

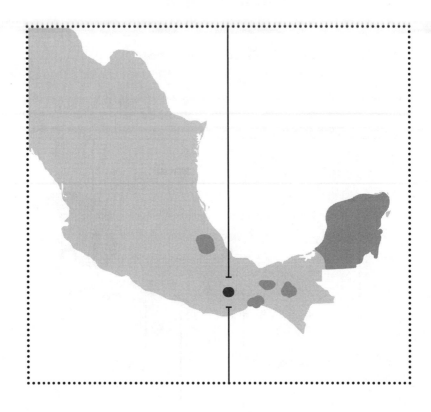

JUAN GREGORIO REGINO

TRANSLATED BY JEROME ROTHENBERG, DAVID SHOOK, JACOB SURPIN, AND ELIOT WEINBERGER

Since the late 1970s, **Juan Gregorio Regino** (b. 1962, Chicicazapa, Oaxaca) has been a leading figure in the movement throughout Latin America charged with the creation of new literatures using native languages alongside the dominant Spanish tongue. A Mazatec by birth and upbringing, Regino was a co-founder and president of the Comité Directivo de Escritores en Lenguas Indígenas [Steering Committee of Writers in Indigenous Languages]. His poetry and other writings have appeared in his own Mazatec and Spanish versions, and in 1996 he received the Netzahualcóyotl Prize for Indigenous Literature. English-language translations of his work have appeared in multiple anthologies and *Words Without Borders.*

In 2005 there were 200,000 speakers of Mazatecan languages, a group of eight closely related languages with varying but generally quite high degrees of mutual intelligibility, in the states of Oaxaca, Veracruz, and Puebla. The language belongs to the Popolocan subgroup of the Oto-Manguean family. Like Zapotec, Mazatec is a Verb-Subject-Object language with tone.

NDIBUA NIJMII

Porque son papeles de juez
Es el libro de tu ley
Es el libro de tu gobierno
Porque puedo hablar con tu águila
Pues nos conoce el juez
Pues nos conoce el mundo
Pues nos conoce Dios
   —María Sabina

I

Nguijíín ndi'í sieen,nguijíín sijen jama ch'aan kojó xka boka,
kia ña tjítí ndi tjingookji'ijña xujun isien nixtjína.
Kji'itie inimána ña tikón né.
Nguixixioma ngatjun nga'ñuu nixtjiin.
Nguitjíbo'á ngaxt'un ndi'ya tsjie.
Ngatajá njñuu ts'uíí kojó sáá,
ngot'e je kókó isieen xi tjijmá ngot'e.

THE SONG BEGINS

Because they are the papers of the judge
It is the Book of your law
It is the Book of your government
Because I know how to speak with your eagle
Because the judge knows us
Because the world knows us
Because God knows us
    —María Sabina

I

In the light of the candle,
In the essence of sweet basil.
In the spirit called forth by the incense,
my life's book is laid out.
Open is my thought before the judge.
The gears of time stop short.
So that Limbo may pull back a pace.
So that the sun and moon dress up
because the images take on a face.

II

Kótso één ndi tjingoonga ts'amijin k'ajmii.
Kotao nijmi xi ya'a nijmeenga tjiejin kjuachikoos'e 'luokasuu
   njñu tjibee.
Ña nguindie,
ña ndiya,kú kó kji›i nga›ñuu chikónxi ts›amejejin isieen najin
   ndi›iieen.
T'iyena ngot'e chjinie.
T'iyena ngot'e nga ts'akutsijennéna,
kó tjindo tistiko.

III

Jí xi yéji kókji'ini ndiyaa ngasundiee.
Jí xi tasín tjéni ngot'e.
Chjux'eni k'ajmii,
takína ngasundiee
Kó chjubenguini
tsi'e nga skue'an kjua chjnie.
Ta'eni kjua nga k'ui'an ndi to xi tjoo.
Takoyéna kótso én xi chja kojó 'bixkiya Néna.
Ngatanguyaji'an nga'ñuu nijmii,
Ngot'e nga s'it'a ja'ína ngasundiee,tiña ndiba isien.
Ñá kjin máni tji›e kojó tjo ndájin.
Tsu'ba nde'an, tsjie'an,ta'eni én,
ta'eni kjuakjintakun.
Nño xi ts'entsijen nguindie ndijo'an.
Ndachikun xi tikon xi xio k'ajmi aso'an.
Nijme xi tsjaa nño t'ananguii kji'anga bojo'an.
Nidi'i xi tsa'boa ndiba isiemba'an.
Naxa ts'uí'an, so'an,kjoacha'an,
nijmi xi ts'endiki'an.

II

What does the smoke of the incese say as it accompanies
the words that initiate their journey to the heavens.
What is the message of the maize your palms propel
that seeks for truth there in the mystery.
In what place, what path
and on what pretext does the guardian of the earth
possess my spirit.
Today reveal it, master:
before my person,
before the eyes of God,
before the witnesses.

III

You who know the sacred,
who lead us on the pathway sown with songs.
Open the sky to me, show me the world,
start me on the path to wisdom.
Let me drink from the childen who spring forth,
teach me to speak and read the language of the Wise Ones,
flood me with the power of the Gods,
inscribe my name there in the Sacred Place.
l am clean, my wings are free.
Dew will cause new words to sprout,
rain will nourish wisdom.
l am star that shines beneath the stone,
sea that dances in the blue of sky,
light that travels in raw weather.
l am sun's vein, l am song.
l am dance and chant that heals.

IV

Ts'akundána isién nixtjín xindájin.
Ngatiandibua numii'en ngot'e,
Nguitijin k'ajmii én xi skjix'a.
Ngatas'ien kjuachikunxi tjijmatjuun chjiniee.
Nguití sien ndi'í tibaa.
Ngatanga jin xi jé jandoo.
Je tjibixkjantje isién nixtjína.
Je tjifichaja'a ndoba isien.
Kia je tsa'bos'ien één chjinie.
Kia je tsa'bos'ien tsja xi mí isieen.
Kia je tsa'bos'ien nijmi xi k'oxie'ána.

V

K'e tikon ndi xka boka ch'ana.
K'e tikon ndi xka boka tsjiena
K'e tikon ndi xka boka xuñona.
Ndi ndiki ch'ana, ndiki tibuana.
Kui kjuajo xi só.
Kui kjuajo xi ndakjan.
Kui kjuajo xi tjitsie
Kui kjuajo xi kjo'on.
Kui xi ya'a nijmi ch'an.
Kui xi ya'a nijmi xuño.
Kui xi ya'a nijmi anda.
Kui xi ya'a nijmi chjinie.

IV

The spirit of evil lies in wait,
the song begins.
May the words arise that open up the heavens,
the prayers that cut across the profance world.
So may the candles of white light be lit
and drip envenomed blood.
It is a mortal struggle in the Sacred Place,
it is the ransom for my spirit.
For my life these fresh leaves will go forth,
these knowing words,
these colored feathers,
these songs for this initiation.

V

Here my basil is at daybreak,
clean like the horizon:
my medicine is fresh,
my medicine is white.
In its leaves the gentle word
that opens up the heavens:
the word that gives us peace,
the word that gives us breath.
My basil will arrive where sins are purged,
will fly off clean to where dawn grows bright.
My pleas will reach into the book of records,
will free my soul from poisons that can kill me.

VI

Kjochó ña tjindo xi nchikunda nixtjiin.
Kjochó ña tjindo xi nchikunda ngaiñuu.
Luichjajo ndoba isien.
Kuichjajo ndoba nixtjien.
Kótjin má ts'ua xi maa ndakjua.
Kótjin ma najin xi maa chja,
xi be ndiyaa k'ajmi,
xi maa chjajo néna.

VII

K'e tikon isien nixtjína.
K'e tikon ndi'ína
K'e tikon nijmina.
K'e tikon nga'ñuna.
Ndaskjanda ndi'ya k'ajmi.
Ndaskjanda ndi'ya tsjie.
Ts'ami'a'an ngo kjuandá.
Ts'ami'a'an ngo kjuajetakún.
Buats'en satikayajin.
Buats'en satíkaya'a.
Ndi'ya ndoba xujun.
Ndi'ya ndoba kjuakjintakun.

VI

My incense will reach the place
where it communes with life.
It will reach the house of those
who are the guardians of the earth.
It will be heard out in the place of images,
will plead its case there in the bosom of the night.
However many mouths they have,
however many tongues they may possess,
those who have knowledge of the heavens,
those conversing with the codices
and speaking with the Gods.

VII

Here is my spirit,
my oak, my cedar.
Here in my heart the prayer is born,
is with it in its journey to the heavens.
From the house of purity,
the table of the dawn.
I am asking for strength.
I am seeking justice.
The sacred book will open,
the darkness will grow bright.
In the house of writings.
In the house of the stelae.

VIII

Ndaskjanda ngaya sé.
Ndaskjanda ngaya tsjá.
Ndaskjanda ngaya xtiin.
Ndaskjanda ngaya ningoo.
Ngat'e kjiya sé.
Ngot'e kjiya tsjá.
Ngot'e kjiya xtiin.
Ngot'e kjiya ningoo.
Ngot'e mána 'bixki nñoo.
Ngot'e mána chjajo'an ndiba isieen.
Ngot'e mána chíkjisun ndoba isieen.
Ngot'e fí nguijin isieen.

IX

Naána Né, na'mína.
Né xi tsa'bojo'an,
yito tjo je ja'atio'an,
yito ngasun k'ajmi iskjitje'anyito kjen xindajin kats'enxi'an.
Ngot'e be nchik'oan nguijin jnuu.
Ngot'e tjína kjuakjitakun tsi'e xi maa kjuaton,
Ngot'e xta xcha xi 'bijña nguii één'an,
chjinie xi sie nga mangase isien nixtjin.
Ndi'ya k'ajmii tsamangasean nijmii,
k'e ts'afoak'ijña chibuan inimana,
ts'afo'a ts'en kja'a kjuakjintalkuun,
ts'amangase'an ndiya tsjie, ndiya xkjuen.

10

VIII

Down to the soles of my feet.
Down to the palms of my hands.
At the apex of my thought.
At the core of my extremities.
My spirit has feet,
my soul has hands,
my veins leave tracks,
pulses of time and the way.
I can talk with the dawn,
submerge myself in turbid waters of torrential rivers,
barefoot can walk up the incline,
can hurl my song against the wind.
I can talk with the dawn,
submerge myself in turbid waters of torrential rivers,
barefoot can walk up the incline,
can hurl my song against the wind.

IX

I arrive with God the Father, God the Mother,
I have crossed seven winds,
seven levels of the heavens.
I have defied seven faces of the World Below.
Because I have eyes for looking at the night,
light enough to plumb the mystery.
Because I am a messenger who guarantees his word,
a singer who can track the soul.
In the house of purity
I come to put my calling to the test,
come to awaken secrets.
I come to seek the word,

Ngot'e nisié xi kjit'usun ngaya isiee'an.
Ngot'e nño xi kjix'a nguindieja'an.
Stra xi siee sába'an.
Ndi xi ts'endaya naxiba'an.

X

K'etjien fé s'uíí,s'ichja ngo ndiya,
fé nijmii.
Nguijin ndi tjingo kis'ijña kjuakjintakun.
Nguijin nijmee s'ichja ngo één,
kó tjo'atjo ni xi ndikon.
Je kamatsijen ngo kjua ndikon,
kja'e ndiya katjux'a.
Nisié xín fítjien,
xún 'bijña t'ananguii.
Sáá tsuya na'mi ts'uina ni xi be ngajñuukó
ndiba isieen je ts'andiba.
K'etjien fé s'uíí,k'etjien ts'enkjaya nijmii,
xtjen kjix'a ndiua tjatsiekó ngasundie tsanguiya ngo kjuandikun.

the fresh path and the clean path.
I am a bird that prophesies the sacred,
morning star that opens the horizon,
cicada that whispers to the moon,
mist that cures the mountain.

X

Here the fiesta ends,
the road is closed, the song is over.
Lucidity is lingering in the copal,
kernels of corn close up their pages,
standing guard over the journey' s secrets.
A mystery is disappearing,
new ways emerging, ways to fathom life.
The birds trace paths, the earth is fasting.
The moon confides her troubles to the sun
and dawn shakes loose on the horizon.
Here the fiesta ends,
the song rests in the morning's arms.
The children who spring forth open the world's heart,
nature is sending signals.

                                                            JR

NIJMI EN NIMA

I

Nijon ochan yoba nga kjín.
Nijon ochan legua k´ajmí,
ndi´í, jñú, isien.
Kiatjien fochó ndaha chjinie,
chjinie xi sié nga tsakihi.
Nguijín isien k´a.
Nguijín isien nguindié.
Nday´a anda anda éhen,
só tsjatsoó,
ndi nijmí ndasen.
Kuíxi fuatjón ndiyahá ngasondié,
ndanga fochó ndobua isien.
Kia chjanijmí,
kia fotí,
kia tsa'boxie´á
nguijín Nena xi nchibotixomá ngasondiéhe.
Tjo ch´ahan 'bitjiyá,
cho´on kjifehe ts´akonda,
bikjín nda´yaní ndaha,
njuijín inimaha ngasondiehe.

II

Xi tsi´e naxi, tsó
xi tsi´e tixa naxi, tsó.
Xi tsi´e xongahá, tsó.
na´míhi tjo ´ñú, tsó.

Xi ts´atsjáná nno, tsó
naan xota nima, tsó.

14

CANTARES

I

Four hundred zontles away,
Four hundred leagues to the endless,
Light, darkness, images.
The voice of the wise one comes from there,
The singer, the soother of woe.
Among the images of the divine,
Among the images of the earth,
His soft voice is heard,
His song of the divine,
His godly prayer.
He crosses over on the path of life,
He travels to the nest of perfect images,
To talk there,
To haggle there,
To plead there
With the gods who rule the fate of the world.
The small wind lulls him,
The sleeping lightning waits for him,
His godly voice echoes like thunder
In the center of the universe.

II

Say lord of the hills.
Say lord of the caves.
Say spirits of the canyons.
Say father of the storm.

Say goddess of fertility.
Say mother of orphans.

Tjian xtjien, tsó.
xi tsi´e ndi´í, tsó.

Tjaha nsié iní, tsó.
yá naxo xán, tsó.
Naxó sijen, tsó.
ndsakuan tsjiun, tsó.

Stse ñanga 'botje ts´uíhi, tsó
ngamasien ngasondiéhe, tsó.
Nangui nda, tsó
nchan ndié nda'ya, tsó.

Ngotjoa ngasondiéhe, tsó
nga´ñú xi k´a ngase, tsó,
Nga ndiboa nga otjé ts´uíhi , tsó.
ngayá isien, tsó.

III

Boats'en tjien nixtjien
buats'en tjien isiehen.
Yito yoba ndojó
yito legua nga kjin.
Kjia tjien focho ndána
kia tjien focho isiená.
Ndi'yaha xota xi ncha tjon
'an xi k'e kjo'a'an,
xi chjinie'an, xi ndiya'an
xi kjit'oso'an.
Ngot'e je katsaéna kjua
ngot'e je tjína kjuakiti
nga kos'ien'an ngaya isien
ñanga kjiyojo xojon ndikon.

Say whore.
Say mistress of fire.

Say macaw feathers.
Say *aguardiente*.
Say fragrant flowers.
Say tobacco dust.

Say rains from the east.
Say center of the world.
Say fertile land.
Say hanging bridges.

Say doors to the shy.
Say greater forces.
Say west and east.
Say place of the images.

III

This is how the day reaches over,
This is how the image reaches over,
Seven leagues away,
Seven zontles to the endless.
From there my voice is heard,
From there my spirit reaches over.
House of the first beings,
I am the one who makes them appear,
I am the wise man, the prophet, the guide,
For I have the permit,
For I have the license
To enter the holy space
Where the wise books are found.
Blessed are you

Néna ngats'enchikonienta'ínjno
nga ngaya tsjien tinchojon.
Ndakochjini tsi'en nga ndiba ngajñu
k'e tjien fo'a ndcok'o'an
k'e tjien fo'a isien nixtjína
kui ndi'ya tjik'iehen
kui ndi'ya ch'ahan.

IV

'An xi chjinie sie'an
'an xi chjinie tsaki'an
'an xi 'boxieji'an isien nixtjin
xi tjindo 'ñu.
¿Ná tikon inimaha?
¿Kó kji'i ni xi kamaha?
'An xi k'oxieji'an
'an xi k'oxie'ahan.
'an xi kamatjiéná.
Ndatsa nguindie nda
ndatsa nguindie ndijo
nguijin isien k'a
nguijin isien nguindie
'an xi kotjojína.
¿Kó kji'i ni xi kamaha?
¿Ñáni nga kistingui?
¿Ñáni nga kistiya?
'An xi k'uindahan
'an xi k'oxieji'an.
Ngot'e jínnáha
ngot'e yojónaha
ngot'e chjinie nda'an
ngot'e mána minchise ndiya
k'e tjien ja'a ndok'o'an

Who dwell in the immaculate house.
We are thankful for the light that lights us.
We are thankful for the night that comes.
From there my footsteps travel,
From there I come,
To this house that offers shade,
To this house that refreshes.

IV

I am the wise singing man,
I am the wise soothing man,
I am the one who drags the captive spirits
From the darkness.
Where is this spirit?
What was it that happened?
I will drag him out,
I will free him,
I will lift him,
I will lift him,
Even if he's underwater,
Even if he's under the rock.
From the images of the sky,
From the images of the earth,
I will set him free.
What is the mistake?
Where is the error?
I've come to bring order,
I've come to do justice,
For it is part of my flesh,
For it is part of my blood,
For I am an honest lawyer,
For I am an explorer on the road.
From there my footsteps travel,

k'e tjien ja'a nijmína,
kjijña isiehen
kjijña nixtjihin.

V

Ndá nguijin inimahan t'ananguihi
ñanga tikon na'minchoana cho'on.
Chja'an ja'ihin, chja'an nixtjihin.
Kjin kjindiboani,
ndojó ndiya xi je ts'atio.
Je soho, je ndakjahan.
Nñojin xi skjiñe
ndajuajin xi k'ui
naminchiboa tsjiehe
na'minchiboa ndikohon.
Ngatjandiboa chjinie xchaha
ngatjandiboa chjinie tjuhun
ngatjandiboa chjinie 'bindaha
ngats'en kas'ien nijmihin.
Kuixi si'in tsjak'iehe inimaha
nga kjuindiba ts'uíhi
nga koja xoñoho
nga kosotjien nixtjihien
kjia stsen sóná
xikoho ngo xtjen.

VI

Ti k'eni tjindojina
ti k'éni tjindo'ahana,
xi tji'e, xi kjinie xota,
xi jó kjen, xi jo isiehen.
Ti k'eni tjindo xi ndojo ningoho

From there my words travel.
The soul is reaching across.
Time is reaching across.

V

From the depths of the earth,
Where our grandfather thunder lives,
I raise his name to call him to his festival.
He comes from far-off times,
He comes from long days.
He's tired, he's wasted,
His food is not tortillas,
His drink is not water,
He is our immaculate grandfather,
He is our grandfather saint.
Let the wise elder come,
Let the wise director come,
Let the wise enchanter come
To deliver our prayers.
That will delight this heart.
When the sun comes,
When the mist clears,
When the day rises,
Our songs will be born
Like cliffs.

VI

They live among us,
They are among us,
The wizards, the man-eaters,
The ones with two faces.
Here are the ones with long fingernails,

xi yito ndijaha.
Ndaha ndi tjingoho k'uitihi:
kuí xi kotíchaya,
kuí xi kjuatjienjó.
Ti k'éni nchikjenjína
ti k'éni tjijmajína,
xi ndirie, xi tji'e
xi ndikonkon, xi ndajin.
K'e tjindo xi tjin najin ndi'í
k'e tjindo xi tjin najin xtí.
Nga´ ñuhun nijminatsí
xi kjo'axín ndiyána,
xi kjo'axín nixtjína.
Ti k'éni tjijmajína
ti k'éni tjijma'ána
xi ndirie, xi ndiá,
xi ndájin, xi ndikonkon.
Ti k'éni tjin xota ndiso
ti k'éni tjindo xi xójo kjuandisoho.
Nga´ ñoho chikon xchaha
xi konga tjinguihi
xi kotíchaya ndiyaha.

VII

Je jachó horaha.
je jachó nixtjíhin.
Buats´en nga ndiba nixtjín
buats´en nga ndibua ndi´í.
Je tjindonda ndastsie
je tikonda kicha
je hora nga si´ankjóho
ndiyá ñá tikon xáná
ndiyá ñá tikon kjuanimáná.

Here the ones with seven horns.
We'll suffocate them with copal smoke.
We'll drag them out,
We'll lift them up.
They eat among us,
They walk among us,
The nahuales, the bewitchers,
The envious, the perverse,
Here are the ones with fire tongues,
Here the ones with tongues that burn.
Only the power of our prayers
Will take them off their road,
Will take them from our lives.
They walk among us,
They're dragged among us,
The transvestites, the incestuous,
The lunatics, the intriguers.
Here are the makers of false literature,
Here the fathers of the lie.
The power of the masters of holy places
Will frighten them from our lands,
Will scatter them from our houses.

VII

The hour has come,
The moment has come.
This is how the day is born,
This is how the light is born.

A *nahual* is a human being capable of physically or spiritually
transforming into an animal. The word has a Nahuatl etymology, but the
concept is common across many indigenous Meso-American cultures.

Je hora nga kjuin
je hora nga x´ianiá.
Tikón stse ch´ahan
tikón na´mi ts´ufuá.
Ndiba ndajua
ndiba sjibé.
Na'mihi xota nguijin jno,
taéná kjondá,
taéná nga´ñú.
Xota ts´enxá´an
tsijen kon ndsa´an,
tjindonguí ndie ningona
ta´éna ngo kjonda nga skungaju´an
nangui xi ijñajne Nena.
Kia kjoáni ni xi xiniejin
kia kjoáni ni xi k´uitjiejin
kia kjoáni naxoó,
yaá, jamaha.
Buats´en nga kjamaxchánijin.
buats ´en nga kjamakjínijin.
Na´mihi xota nguijin jno,
taéná kjonda,
taéná kjuoatjó
xota ts´enxá´an.
Ndandabuáha xi kjijin k´e´an
ndase xi yi´á ndso'ba´an
ni tjién xi tjiyá ndsa´an
inima xi tjiyá ndsa´an.

The bowl is ready,
The machete is ready,
It is the time to think
On the place of our work,
On the place where our power is.
It is the hour of leaving,
It is the hour of beginning.
Here is the new rain,
Here is father sun.
The water falls,
The heat falls.
Patron San Isidro,
Grant me permission,
Grant me authority.
I work in the fields,
There are creases in my hands,
There is dirt in my fingernails.
Let me touch the earth
That the great God left us.
From there my food will come,
From there my seed will come,
From there my flowers, my trees,
My roots will come.
That is how we grow,
That is how we are multiplied.
Lord San Isidro,
Grant me your grace,
Grant me your favor.
I work in the fields,
There is sweat on my face,
There is mud on my clothes,
There is a seed in my hand,
There is life in my hand.

VIII

Án xi kjo'e'an ngot'e,
kó kji'í kienu
kó kji'í isiehen.
'An xi ts'achjaji'an
án xi ts'achja'a'an.
Naan tsjen
naan chiki
naan xuño
naan t'anangui
naan yiboa.
Jí xi jun ik'ijniji chiboa
jí xi jun ik'ijniji ndiya.
Nana jun
nana xcha.
'Énri xi 'ñu k'a tsu'ba
kui ngasondie nijmehe.
Kui ngasondie ndáha.
Jí xi chánji
jí xi xuñoji.
Ngayá ndse
ngayá ningoho
kamá tajá yáha
kama tajá ndijoho
katjux'a k'ajmihi
kjindibá sahá
kjindiba nñoho
Ngoté jí xi kini'inji
ngot'e jí xi ik'ichjéji
xota xi jnóho
xota xi nk'ien.
Jí xi katsaéjne isien.
Jí xi katsaéjen ndi'í.

VIII

Now I am here before you.
What is your face like?
What is your soul like?
It is I who invokes you,
It is I who implores you.
Mother milk,
Mother breasts,
Mother mist,
Mother earth,
Mother zontle.
You left the first footprint,
You made the first step.
Ancient mother,
Grandmother.
Your prayer is the highest
In this world of corn,
In this world of water,
In this rich world.
Your are the cool breeze,
You are the mist,
Between your hands,
Between your fingers,
The tree grows hard,
The rock grows hard,
The sky opens,
The moon blossoms,
The stars appear,
For you have come,
For you have blocked
The demons who lived before there was light
And the demons who live in hell.
You gave us light,

Nana ndiyá
nana 'na
nana 'yo.
Jí xi ik'ijniji chiboa
jí xi ik'ijniji xtihin.
¡Ngatamachikoniéji!
Santísima Trinidad.

IX

K'e tikon ndi tjingo sijéna
k'e tikon k'io chj'ina
k'e tikon ndiki ch'ana
k'e tikon tsa inína xi fí k'ajan
k'e tjindo, k'e ts'enkas'ie'an.
Kui chjí xi ts'atsjaha
tsi'e kjondá xi tini'ína
tsi'enga ts'akongajo'an yojoho.
Nguijin yojoho kjamaxchaji'an
nguijín yojoho tikonjián.
Tjits'en jmahan ndsa'an
nga tjits'eo'hon yojoho.
Ngot'e boats'en je íjña néná
ngot'e boatso kjuakitihi.
Yojohori kjotjojin nñona
yojohori kjotjojin ndáná.
Chí tsehe,
chi tsa'án.
Bojóri ndatsaji
xindari ndtasaji.
K'e tikon kjuanimana
k'e ndandabúana

28

You gave us fire,
Guide mother,
Luminous mother,
Sprout mother.
You left the first footprint,
You made the first step.
You are holy,
Blessed trinity.

IX

Here is my sweet-smelling incense,
Here are my best cacao beans,
Here is my fresh medicine,
Here is my feather that rises.
Take them, they are for you.
It is the payment for allowing me,
For giving me permission,
To touch your body,
I grow on your body,
I live on your body,
I have stained my hands
Striking your body.
This is how God has arranged it,
This is how God has ordered it.
My food will come from you,
My drink will come from you.
A little for you,
A little for me.
You too are hungry,
You too are thirsty.
Here is my offering,
Here is my thankfulness.

jíínji, chobeji,
kuí xi tsjaha nga'ñu
kuí xi tsjaha inimaha.

X

K'e tikón mdi'í si'en'a
k'e tjitína sien tibána.
Boats'en nga mi'ahan nga'ñu.
boats'en nga mi'ahan ngo kjoandá.
Kóts'en kjonguina yojona
kóts'en kojáná nixtjin.
Ñáni nga tikon xi ch'an
ñáni nga tikon xi 'yo
ñáni nga tikon ndiyaha
ñáni nga tikon kjua kixihi.
Boats'en nga mi'a'an ngo nga´ñu
boats'en nga mia'a'an ngo kjonda.
Jí xi na'miji
jí xi naanji
ti'íntsjijina, ti'ínchit'ena,
ti'ínchikonína, tasíngandiyéna.
K'e tjitína ndi'í siéná
k'e tikon sien tibána.

XI

Kjua nima, kjua tjoho
ja'a'an ndoba isien.
K'uindajíbora'an ngot'e
nguijín isien nixtjihin.
K'uindabora'an ngot'e
míra xi ndájin kji'i.
Kamána, s'indajína

Drink it, take it,
It will give you strength,
It will give you life.

X

With my light burning,
With my white candle lit,
This is how I ask for strength,
This is how I ask for mercy.
How will I survive?
How will I live out my days?
Where is calmness?
Where is coolness?
Where is the path?
Where is truth?
This is how I ask for strength,
This is how I ask for mercy.
You who are the father,
You who are the mother,
Cleanse me, bless me.
Protect me, show me the way.
Here I bring my burning light,
Here I bring my white candle.

XI

With sacrifices, with humility,
I have reached the nest of perfect images.
I will restore the order
Inside your body,
I will repair the error
In what surrounds you.
Yes I will cure you,

sokóna, kamandayána.
Ngot'e je boats'en katsaéna
ngot'e je bosts'en ik'ijñána.
Kó kji'i ni xi kamaha
ñá tikon isien nixtjihin
'yá xi tikon'ñoho
a chikón ngotjaba
a chikón tjinguiba
'yá xi katsanguiya
xi íjña 'ñu ndoba isien.
An xi kamána ko'naxiéjin
an xi kamána kongase ndiyaha.
A tjin xi chíchja tjinguihi
a kjuaxtí tjingojin inimaha.
'an xi kotjikjaya'an
'an xi kotijet'a'an.
Ñá tikon ñanga tsaka
ñá tikon ñanga kistinguihi.

Yes I will mend you,
For that is what has been given me,
For that is what has been granted me.
What was it that happened?
Where is your soul?
Where is your spirit?
Who holds you captive?
Is it the master of the door?
Is it the master of the hill?
Is it someone who has sent you
To be punished in the nest of perfect images?
Yes I will set you free,
Yes I will light your way.
Is there envy?
Is there malice?
Is there anger?
I will restore order,
I will make peace
Where the fault is,
Where the error is.

EW

CHJUNNÁ

Tsie kjuakjintakun xi ya'a chjunná,
ndanga s'e, katsenjóni,
nguijin inimaa kojó naxaa tikónji.
Fíjin isieen nixtjiin,
ngasema 'ñu ngasemá nga ko'a tsuíí.
Tsakjonjin xi ndoba kojó xi ch'an.
Tsa nguijin tjoo, kojótsa nguijin ndi'í.
Tasáma tingá kjuakjintakuun.
Fo'axin kjua ndasena,
fo'atjo yojona nga je jinda'an.
Tsie kjuakjintakun xi ya'a chjunna
nguijin naxaa kojó ngaya inima tikon 'ma,
ko tikón chikin chikin xikotsa ngo yákun,
xikotsa ngo ndijo nga tjiyá inimána.

34

MY WOMAN

My woman has a strange power—
it grew with her since she was small,
carried in her bones and veins.
Her face never pales,
it grows stronger with the sun.
Her heart does not grieve,
it has life by day and night.
Between the fire and the cold,
the flame of her tenderness
eases my sadness,
blankets my humanity.
My woman has a strange power—
It hides in her blood and on her skin
it makes her firm, like a statue
and she is like an oak in my heart.

JS

BE' AN ÉHÉN NGASONDIE

Jé ts´afuatjiyajóna ngasondie,
Jé ts´akílx´ána ngatlua,
t´ie yejé´an ´yá xi chja,
xi mojnó, xi kjanda.
Bé yije´an kó kji´í ngasondie.
Kuixi ts´afoatjiyajóna,
xi ts´abokóna, xi se´enchjajóna.
Ngat´e be´an éhén ngasondie.
Ngat´e be´an éhén naxihi.
Ngat´e be´an éhén chohon
Ngatjandibua nisié´ne.
Ngatjandibua xundaxi´í´ne.
Ngisiejóna.
Ngatjaa tjingo bojón´e.
Ngatjaá tsjiun´e.
Ngat´e be´an éhén yáhá.
Ngat´e be ´an éhén ts´uíhi.
Ngat´e be án éhén ndijoho.
Ngat´e be´an éhén t´anangui.
Ngat´e be´an éhén naxoho.
Ngat ´e be´an éhén nixtjiehen.
Ngat´e be´an éhén nñoho.
Ngat´e be ´ an éhén sáhá.
Ngat´e be´an éhén kjaboyáha.
Ngat´e be´an éhén choho.
Ngat´e be´an éhén inimaha.
Ngatjandibua naxón´e.
Ngatja´a k´ion´e
Nguit´iénan´e
Nguit´iénan é
Kuíxi kamá chik´o´an,
Kuíxi kamá yibina

36

I KNOW THE WORLD'S TONGUE

The world now spins with me,
now opens her doors to me.
I can hear those who talk,
who laugh, who cry.
I discover the world's mystery.
The world now spins with me,
teaches me and talks to me.
Because I know the world's tongue.
Because I know the tongue of the hillside,
the thunder, the tree and the day.
Because I know the sun's tongue.
Because I know the tongue of the stone,
of the earth, of the flower and of the night.
Because I know the star's tongue.
I know the tongue of the moon,
of the cloud, of the sea and of death.
May the flowers now come.
May the birds now come.
May the roosters now come.
May they sing with me.
May the copal now come.
May the tobacco now come.
May the cacao now come,
may they listen to me.
They will be my guardians.
They will be the keys
that will open the doors for me.
They will guard me
in the clear, in the visible,
in the dark and the shadows.
They will be my guardians.

DS

Xi skjix´ ána ngatjua.
Kuíxi skona
Ñanga tsijen, ñanga nixtjien,
Ñanga iñó, ñanga tiik 'ien,
Kuí kama nchik´oan.

ZOQUE

CHIAPAS • MEXICO

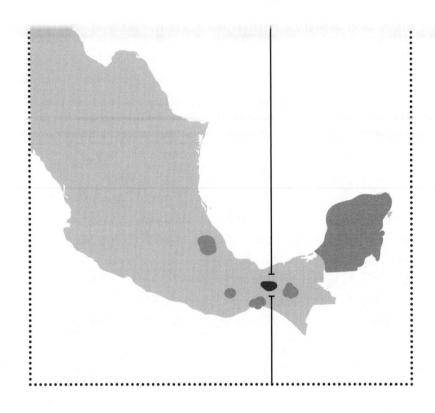

MIKEAS SÁNCHEZ

TRANSLATED BY DAVID SHOOK

Mikeas Sánchez (b. 1980) writes poetry and fiction in the Zoque language of Chiapas. She has published five books of poetry. Sánchez is currently director of XECOPA, an indigenous radio station in Chiapas. English-language translations of her poems have appeared in *Bengal Lights*, *World Literature Today*, *The Bitter Oleander*, and *The Drunken Boat*. Her work was nominated for a 2014 Pushcart Prize.

The Zoque languages form a branch of the Mixe-Zoquean language family, spoken by some 70,000 people in the Southern Mexican states of Chiapas, Oaxaca, and Tabasco. Chiapas Zoque is a Verb-Subject-Object language without tone, characterized by long words and its use of affixes and clitics. Zoque is an endangered language due to the rapid shift to Spanish among Zoque youths, though this is being actively combated by language activists like Sánchez, who broadcasts radio programming in the language.

JESUCRISTO'IS JA' ÑÄJKTYÄJ'YA ÄJ' TZUMAMA'IS KYIONUKSKU'Y

Äj' tzumama'is ja' myuspäkä' kastiva'ore
natzu' jyambä'ä ngyomis'kyionukskutyam
natzu' xaä' tumä nabdzu'
jyambäukam yanuku'is musokiu'tyam
Äj' tzumama'is wyanjambana' jujche' ore'omorire'na
Muspabä tä' tzamä'sawa'jin
tese' kujtnebya'na eyabä' ngomis wyinan'omoram
tese'na konukspa chokoyjin ni'ijse
Jesucristo'is ja' myajna kyonujksku'y
te' yore äj' dzumamas'ñye
ñä' ijtu'na pomarrosas yoma'ram
tese' sunkbana' tumä' matza
wyrün'omoram wadbasenaka'
San Miguel Arkangel'is ja' myajna' kyänuksku'y
äj'tzumama'is kyänuksku'y wenen'omo yaxonguy'tyam'dena'
jukis'tyt numbana' tese' poyajpana te' toya'ram
patsoke wejpana' tese' te' Sungä mita'na yängu'kyämä
Te' yängu'kyämärike pänayaju' kuyay'yune'ram

42

JESUS NEVER UNDERSTOOD MY GRANDMOTHER'S PRAYERS

My grandmother never learned Spanish
was afraid of forgetting her gods
was afraid of waking up in the morning
without the prodigals of her offspring in her memory
My grandmother believed that you could only
talk to the wind in Zoque
but she kneeled before the saints
and prayed with more fervor than anyone
Jesus never heard her
my grandmother's tongue
smelled like rose apples
and her eyes lit up when she sang
with the brightness of a star
Saint Michael Archangel never heard her
my grandmother's prayers were sometimes blasphemies
jukis'tyt she said and the pain stopped
patsoke she yelled and time paused beneath her bed
In that same bed she birthed her seven sons

——————————

Jukis'tyt and *patsoke* are Zoque swear words.

NEREYDA'IS MYABAXÄYU NWYT NEW'YORK

Nereyda'is myabaxäyu nwyt New'York
ne' yamumä' kiene tumä tuku' ma'aomo ñoyibäis Macy's
tumä ore'yomo
tumä pabiñomo pänajubä' dä' najsomo'ram
tumä' nkiae ne' pyoyubä koxtaksi'
ne' chajkienbäu'bäis dyagbajk'ajku'y
Yanu'ku'is myuja'ajkujxye'
jaya' iri' nijuräbä kubgu'y nasakobajk'omo
yäjse' tejse' yenu' ojse'jin
te' nkiäram takyajubä pakakis'
kawa' wä' yispüjkiaju te' tzama ja' yispäjkia'äjse xis'
jiksek' Ngiomi te' nasakobajk'
Tzitzungätzäjk'mäbä
Tumä mätzik' wane'rire'na
juwä' yagbajk'unestam' wyä'ñayajpana ñyatzku'tyam
Teje te Pinakate jenere'na natzkuxebä'
Tumä ne'pyakäyubä' pabiñomo'koroya
teje' te tojtzubä'najs Sonorasñye' jenere'na mujabä'
wäkä pyatayaä' pyajk' käwanubä poyo'omoram
Nereyda'is myabaxäyu nwyt New'York
ne' yamumä' kiene tumä tuku' ma'aomo ñoyibäis Macy's
Nasakobajk' uka mujspa manä'
minä' pinja' yanima
minä' yajk' tzunja' kyändätzä' tumä'moneko' majkis yames'ñye
minä' nobujta' dyajxu'tzujkayajubä' xys'
minä' yajk' tujkwiruä kyae'omo
te' kyae' myätzäbya'bäsna tzaune'ram
ijtyajubä te' tzitzungätzojkis'myeya'omo
minä' tejin' käminä'
minä'

NEREYDA DREAMED IN NEW YORK

Nereyda dreamed in New York
contemplating her reflection in a Macy's window
a migrant ore'yomo
a girl born in the Tzitzun empire
a girl fleeing barefoot
as far away as possible from orphanhood
The grandness of her lineage could never
be compared to any other kingdom
but she grew up hungry
and her hands chapped by the cold
knew the countryside better than they know her own body
so Nasakobajk from the majesty of the Tzitzungätzojk
was just a music box
where the orphan girls stored their fear
But the Pinacate was too rural
for a cold girl
but the Sonora desert was very big
to find her skeleton hunched among the dunes
Nereyda dreamed in New York
contemplating her reflection in a Macy's window
Oh Nasakobajk if you can hear her
draw near to gather her soul
draw near to satiate her 500-year thirst
draw near to rescue her injured body
draw near to turn her back into a girl
the one that played with the pebbles
that surround Tzitzun's crater
draw near to her
draw near

TE' KOJAMA WIRUBA' JANA
TZAME'IS WYEJKUY'OMO

I

Te' kojama wiruba' jana tzame'is wyejkuy'omo
        wiruba' wäkä yukä' nä'
yajubäjin wynabä kyändotzä
nä' jurä' nasakobajkis kyojtpäu myusokiu'y
nä' kana'paajpä jurä' dä' ngomi'is chyajku xyijs'sis yoma'
Te' kojama'is ñäbujtpa ñatzku'y
        ñäbujt'pa kyajsojkuy
mietzpa poyo'is xyängä
mietzpa tum'iri'is jyuwi'
Tese' te' wyrän'nä' mutpa tuj'omoram
mutpa' wyndutzi'omo
jurä' dä' amyajpa kaya'jubä

III

Nä' ijtützi jana'tzame äj' ngojama'omo
anäbyabä' tujin'
Tese' te' toya saba' äj' wirän'akña'omo
tese poñi'boñi maka jamobyabä äj' wyrän'omo
kukosobya' kotzäjk'käjsi
nkyps'pa äj' achpä'jara'is pyeka'iri'omo
—äj' nkojama'is yätzpäba' sabila teserike takabyä'ajy—
Te' toya' maka' kujk'tzu'omo
kujk' poya'omo

SELECTIONS FROM
The Soul Returns to the Shout of Silence

I

The soul returns to the shout of silence
  returns to drink seawater
with which it satiated its first thirst
water of life where the earth deposited its Arcanum
water of such sweet saltpeter where God left essences of his body

The soul discards mysticism
  discards hope
seeks reflections of sand
seeks embers of solitude
And its eye of water sprouts in drops of rain
in the corner of the eye
to see ghosts

III

The soul emanates perfumes
exhales secrets of the species
revitalizes the remote regions of my pains
searches for an obolus of peace
  over hills of sleep
traces spheres of tenderness
  to compensate for solitudes

My soul
amethyst orchid seeking water
  water of ancient coconut
as ancient as pain

VII

Nä' ijtutzi jana'tzame äj' nkojama'omo
anälyabä krjpak' tuj'
Tese' te' tum'ijtkuy sa'ba äj' wirün'akña'omo
                    [wäkä myawä' jamobyabä äj' wyrän'omo
kuko'sobya kotsäjk'käjsi
nkyps'pa äj' anuku'is yijtkuy'omoram
—aj' nkojama'is yäts'päba' sabila teserike ajenju—
Tese' te' tum'ijtkuy sirijtpa kujktzu'omo
                    [kujk' nana'luna'omo

X

Äj' jame yäjk'pä jame're
                    [jinam mabä' wyrui'
¿Jujtxye' muspatzi nukä' ijtumä' meya'nä'
                    [nä'kana'paajpä
¿Jujtxye' yajpa' yä' notkuy?
äj' ngäram' takyajpa npikpakäjtzi te' nä'
i'makste' äjtzi' ji' nakste' äj' te' toya
äjtzäj'xyä te' yäjkpä'perla yajkaoye'is wyrän'omobä
Tese' metzpatzi äj' jara, metzabiatzi puabä'kyasäjk'kuy

VII

I have silences in my soul
rustling with the rain
and solitude dawns from my left eye
                    [to my right eye
spy since volcanic cycles
meditates from the windows of my grandparents
—Vomits sage and wormwood—
Solitude is freed at midnight
                         [at moon's marrow

X

My memory is the black box
            [of a plane without return
How did it reach the libation of sea water
                    [of such sweet saltpeter?
How do I justify this extravagant intoxication?
my hands shatter in contact to water
who am I if not the counterpoint of pain
the black pearl in the eyes of the suicide
and I look for my father and his withered joy

XV

Te' winabä äj' ndäjk'omo
manhatzi te' nä'is yoitzkuy'
tese' muspatzi jujche jinde' te' meya'is nä tzamebä'
tujte' kejkpa täjkäsi
Mindyä'tzum te' "tuj'poya"
mumu' dä' mujs'tamba jujchere' makabä' mujyae dä' ngoso'ram

Ägba'mätzi yäti' jinam' kieke' tuj'
ji' kieke' nä'
   ji' kieke' jap
      ji kieke' poyo'
sona'ri're' dä' manba
jayeram' sänyajpabä maais'ñyeram
Ägba'mätsi yäti'
jairäm' äj' achpä'jara
akuajkubä' wyrän'jin
metza'ora nabdzu'is'ñyeomo

XVI

Ne' sutu' nwyrä' tandan'jin
            [wäkä mujsä' ngäwä' te' tzajp
ne' sutu' ndumä' äj' jana'tzame
            [meya'ubu'is nwyaj'yin
ne' sutu' mbarä' meya'is chyokoy
juwä' tyokoya'jumä sukxya'ubä
teserike mietxyajpabämä' aa'bänis'tam
            [nüa'yomo'is wyane'omo
¿Juwä'a' makiajpa' te' pobo'rambä' tandan
kyukiaj'pabäis te' tzajp?
¿juwä'a' nukpa' te' kojama'peyase'wejpabä?

50

XV

From the house that I'm not at
I hear the dancing of the waves
and it's not the sea that speaks to me
it's the rain that slaps the roof
The north wind has arrived
and we all know that our feet will get wet

Where I sleep it no longer rains
Not even drops of water
   or silica
      or sand
only the noises of cars
signs and neon lights
Where I sleep
my grandfather no longer
opens his naked eyes
at two in the morning.

XVI

I want to go on a pilgrimage with butterflies
               [and upholster the sky
I want to unite my silence
               [with the waves' hair
I want to find the heart of the sea
that the drowned lost
and that navigators keep hunting
               [in mermaids' songs
Where do the white butterflies that
upholster the sky migrate?
where do the soul and its falcon's shriek reach?

XVII

Äj' nkojama jekä're
ɉı' nc' nkyatyou'bäsñyc'
te' nä'xyka tajsubä
    [oktubre poya'omo
te' nä'tzika' ijtpamä te' anksän
        [teserike' te'nä' ichi'ram

Äjchomä' ijtu te' muso'kiuy winabä tza'isñye'
tese metspatsi äj' ndzokoy' mosabyä mabaxi'omo
   metzpatzi te' tokoyubä mabaxi' äj' anuku'is´ ñyeram
      te' yajkxu'ijtkuy tä' karam'babä'omo
           [mitaj'se'naka sawa'is xyukuy'

XVII

My soul is the last agony
of the regretful suicide
the pitcher that filled with rain
            [on October afternoons
the water of the well where time lives
                [and its marine monsters

I am the chimera of marble's secrets
and I seek my heart in the fifth game of lethargy
    I seek that lost dream of my ancestors
            this solitude of dying life
                        [in each kiss of the wind

Maka mini' te' kaku'y
tese maka mbyare' mij' änguy'omo
maka mbyare' mij' dujkijs myuka'omora'm
jiksekande te' yäjk'pii tandanijs
makabä chyajme jujche maka ngiae
Jiksekande' makabä jambä'i mij' näyi'
maka dyuki' tumä mabaxi'
te' mabaxi ja' tyujkäbä tzayi'kam
u te' mabaxi yagbajk'unes'ñye
tese ñyagbajk'une mareke' mijtzi

Death will arrive
and it will find you in your bed
amid the fungus that occupies your house
or in the memory of the black butterfly
that anticipates your absence
Then you will forget your name
and you will become a dream again
the dream of an afternoon never contemplated
or the dream of the street child that you once were
and have not ceased being

Maka mini te' kaku'y
te' wiyun'sebä
    te' tä' tochäjk'pabä'is
maka' wyajtayae mij'ngäi a'm
maka' ñdyok'mäni' muja'pitzu'omo
jiksekande makabä mujsi'
jujche ijtyaju jäkia'jubä surä'
tem'dyemä wänbamä mij' ndoya

Death will arrive
the true one
    the tyrant
she will bind your hands
she will toss you into the abyss
and only then will you know
that there are deeper voids
than the solitude you keep

Wäkä dä' jambä'ä te' toya'
wä' tü konuksä'
wäkä' tä' jambä'oya
wä' dä' jambä'ä te' toya
dä' bajkomo'angaspä
Yajk' yaä' te kakuyis'
jyame
Pijstin'omo yajk' wiru'ä
äj› anima
Wäkä' jambä'ä te' toya'
wäri' jambä'ä äj' näyi'

To forget pain
just one prayer is enough
for forgottenness
pain compresses
deeper in my bones
To erase the memory
of my death
that my soul become
a Ceiba
to forget pain
forgetting my name is enough

RAMA

Te' sudgu'y tumä pajk'te jairäbä'is ñyoyi'
—Julieta Valero

Jojpajkin tajsu'xys
jojpajk kutpa yuñ'ijtkuy'omo dyom'ijtkuy'omo
ñä' ijtu' ips' komajk komojsay ame'
teje' ñä' ijtpa patsoke'une
tekoroya jyokpa jyaya
joyä tsäkibä' yasa'kämä
sudgu'y kämä'
poñi'bä konukskuy'jin
konukspä tsu' ko' tsu'
wäkä myajkpä'ä sudguy'istyoya'

Kasujpa tä' ägba' jana'pama
uka' ni'ijs ji' tä' ägba' jana'pama
uka' ni'ijs ji' tä' pike' dä yomijtku'y
teje' nkipspa' sone'naka
yangamyajpasen'omo wyrun'dam
teje' myabaxäbya' Dakar'pä kubgu'y
juwä sone' yujk'tambä yomo'istam
ne' pyojkin'dchokiaju pyabiñomo'ajkutyam
tumdumäbä'is wyadba peka'wane wolof'ore'omo
tumdumäbä pabiñomo nä' jonchire'
ne' xirijtubä sudguy' käjsi

RAMA

Desire is a bone that no one's named.
　　—Julieta Valero

The rivers that inhabit her
branch off between her infancy and sex
she is thirty-five years old
and knows that Mahoma will not forgive her
a son without a father
so her womb calmly waits
beneath her flowered dress
beneath passion
from a silent prayer
that she utters each night
to drive away the discomfort of the flesh

To be free is to sleep naked
without hands seeking your sex
she thinks a thousand times
while she closes her eyes
and dreams she's on a street in Dakar
with a dozen young black women
newly arrived at puberty
each one rehearses ancestral canticles in Wolof
each one is a wild gull
circling desire

AISHA'

Kyä'wänba tyojtskämä
te' takabyäoma' dyomo'alkuy'lsñye'
te' España te' Marruecos
tere' tumä' pabiñomo juka'bätzäbä
tijan chan'gabä
suñi'tyambü'iswyrändam
Chajku' Marrakech
dä' mboyaj'biajse dä ngämung
dä' mboya'yajpajse sungä'ram tajsubä'luna'ram Hachís'oma
tzutsibü'nä'oma
dä' sukpa' tyäjkmä dä' sukpa ñyaka'omo

Myama'is chajmayu
jana' tyena' tome' näkät'numba'mä jana' tyena' tome'
moch'andun'mä' jana' tyena' tome' sudguy'mä myama'is
    kyät'chiu'
te' takabyä' oma' tyojtzijs'ñye'
Mumure' tä' yäjktambä
te' jawakiu'y chyejkis'ñye' yomo'ankä'ne' jyoku'bäis winabä'
    jyaya'

Hachís'oma kanela'oma
maka' yajk' soje' kyäräjk' asa'käjsi
wäkä' te' jyaya'is jana' kyomujsa'
eyarambä' pänis'yoma wänubä ñaka'omo Hachís'oma
hierbabuena'oma
maka' chi'i myama'
wäkä' chejk'omo dyen'a tumä une'
hachís'oma kanela'oma
wäkä' ngyomi' Ala'is chiä' tumä nga'e
wäkä 'ngyomi'Ala'is myasan'äjya jyaya'is tyämbu'

AISHA

Guards the bitter sensation of her sex
beneath her tongue
in Spain as in Morocco
keeps being the coppery girl
with wide hips
and exact eyes
She left Marrakesh
like someone fleeing their own shadow
she avoids streetlamps and the full moon
In her house and on her skin
the scent of green tea and hashish

Her mother warned her of the dangers
of going too close to bridges
and balconies
and loves
her mother shared
the bitter sensation on the tongue
the ardor in her belly
of a woman saving herself for her first love

Scent of hashish and cinnamon
will anoint her wedding dress
so that her groom doesn't reveal
the scent that her skin guards from other men
Scent of hashish and peppermint
she will offer to her mother
so that her belly fosters a child
scent of hashish and cinnamon
so that Allah will give her a child
so that Allah will bless her man's seed

EASTERN HUASTECA NAHUATL

VERACRUZ • MEXICO

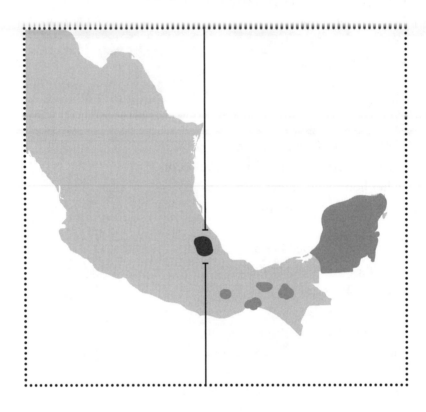

JUAN HERNÁNDEZ RAMÍREZ

TRANSLATED BY ADAM W. COON AND DAVID SHOOK

Juan Hernández Ramírez (b. 1951, Colatlán, Veracruz) has published five books of poetry in Eastern Huasteca Nahuatl, including *Chikome Xochitl* [*Seven Flower*], which won the 2006 Nezahualcóyotl Prize for Indigenous Literature. Hernández Ramírez writes simultaneously in Nahuatl and Spanish, using the languages, in his own words, as mirrors, a process representative of how many contemporary indigenous Mexicans live and work between languages.

The Nahuatl language family is spoken by 1.5 million contemporary Mexicans, making it the largest indigenous language of North America. As part of the Uto-Aztecan family it is a distant relative to Native American languages Comanche and Hopi. Huasteca Nahuatl is divided into 3 groups with high mutual intelligibility, and is spoken by nearly 1 million of the language's 1.5 million speakers. Nahuatl is a Subject-Verb-Object language notable for its long words created by affixing. The Classical Nahuatl of the Mexican Aztecs is roughly as far removed from contemporary Nahuatl as our English is from Shakespeare's, though somewhat closer to the Central Nahuatl dialects than to Huasteca Nahuatl. Juan Hernández Ramírez' poetry claims a clear lineage from the flower singers of Classical Nahuatl poetry, affirming the historical Mexican identity of the contemporary Nahuatl speaker.

MIAUAXOCHITL

I

Ipan ueyatl axiuitik sintli
Makuilxochitl kipatlaua imamal.

Kueponi miauatl.

Xali xochitl tiokuitlatik

In ajuechkali
moxochitlakentijok.

San eltok kuikatl tlatsotsontil.

MAIZE FLOWER

I

Tender green corn upon the great sea.
Makuilxochitl unloads her shawl.

The barbed corn blooms.

Gilded sand flower.

The house of dew
is dressed with flowers.

Only hymns and holy melodies.

Makuilxochitl ("Five Flower") is a pre-Columbian reference to a female
Nahua poet from the fourteenth century and the patron god of writing
and painting.

II

Tlilelemeka tonatij itsonkal
ipan sintli itlakayo.

Moxochiotlaltok Xilonen.

Pankistok siltik tlilelemektli.

Tlixochitl
toselik nakayo.

Ketsalxochimej kali.

II

The sun's hair flames
over the body of maize.

Xilonen has blossomed.

The small-grained flame has sprung.

Flower of fire
our tender flesh.

House of precious flowers.

Xilonen, or *xilotl* (*jilote* in Spanish or "green spike of maize"), refers to
when the kernels of Chikomexochitl (the "Seven Flower" of the book's
title) are soft and just beginning to bud. Xilonen is also a pre-Columbian
reference to the feminine side of Centeotl ("maize god," which appears in
the following poem).

III

Chichiltik, yayauik, chipauk, kostik
ikuctlaxo itlapoyauilis.

Tlen sintli tlayoli.

Ika xochitl mokuachijtok Senteotl.

Kuika miauatototl.

In chalchiuitl uitsitsilij,
ika xochitl moiuintia.

III

Red, black, white, yellow
the hues of her skin.

Choice kernel of corn.

Centeotl adorns her head with flowers.

The blossoming maize flower sings.

The jaded hummingbird,
drunken with flowers.

IV

Kostik xochitl tlaixpaj.
Kantelaj tlauili. Kopalij ipokyo

Tokistli tiochiualistli.

Tlali, se uinoj tlatsikuintli,
inik tlakatl seyok.

Xochimej, inik matlaeli.

Tlapojtok tlali, tlaoli kiselia.

IV

Yellow flowers on the altar
Candle light. Copal smoke.

Sowing consecrated.

For earth, one offering of drink,
for man, another.

For abundance, flowers.

Earth open, it receives the choice seed.

V

Ipan youali tlakoyoyan kochki,

ajuechtli kiauitl issa.

Sintoktli.

Ipan kalejekatl yoltok.

Ipan tlauitlalpan moskaltia,
xochiketsal ikuaxanko.

Xoxoktik xiuitl papalotl.

V

It slept in night's furrow.

Rain's dew awakes.

The corn stalk.

It lives in the wind's house.

It grows in the land of light,
in Xochiquetzal's bossom.

Green leaves like a butterfly.

Xochiquetzal ("flowery quetzal bird" or "flowery preciousness") is a
pre-Columbian allusion to the patron goddess of the arts.

VI

Ketsaltotol kitlalana ipatlanil,
uiuipika sintli ixoutyo

Ipan xoxouik xopantla tlali
tlen tlauili kuauitl moskaltia.

Kuikaya Xochitototl.

Tlapouij xiuimej
ipan yolistli.

VI

The quetzal lifts into flight,
the maize leaf shudders.

In the green earth of rainy season
the tree of light grows.

The flower bird already sings.

Leaves open
to life.

VII

Ipan tonatij ichaj yoltok.

Tlen yolistli tiokuitlatl yoltok,
kostik sintlayoli.

Xoxoktik mestli xiuimej
itsajla tiotlatik tlauili uiuipikaj.

Tsaktok xochikoskatl.

Panlantok uitsitsilij.

VII

Corn-child lives in the sun's house.

Life's living gold,
yellow seed of corn.

Green moon leaves
tremble beneath the afternoon light.

The necklace of flowers is complete.

The hummingbird has flown.

I

Choloua tsintlayouali.

Kueponi xochitl.

Tlali kuika.

Motektok xochitl,

moilpiaj,

motlaixpaj tlaliaj,

Sinteotl xochitl itlamauisol.

SOWN FLOWER

I

Night flees.

The flower emerges.

Earth sings.

The flowers are cut.

Strung together.

Offered up.

Centeotl is the flower's miracle.

II

Tlatokxochitl.

Inik sintli popochtli,
xochitl tlatiochiuali.

In xochiatl,
ika ejekatl timijtotia.

Totiotsij sintlakatl tikajuiyalia.
Tonantsij sinsiuatl tikajuiyalia.

II

Sown flower.

Copal for the corn,
flower's prayer.

Liquid flower,
you dance with the wind.

You perfume Father Corn.
You perfume Mother Corn.

III

Tlikuauitl,
ıstakmeatlı tıjtlikuiltia.

ljkiti xochitl tlanestli.

Akosemalotl in tlaijkitijketl
Ipan kuauitl kipa xochitl.

Tlapaltik kiauitl.

Kiauitl xochipetlatl.

III

Tree of fire,
you light up the moon.

The morning weaves flowers.

The rainbow's weaver
paints flowers on the tree.

Colorful rain.

Petals of rain.

IV

Ichpochiotik chichiuali,
ajuechtli xochimimili.

Tepitsin mestli iajuiyakayo.

Tlen xopantla moxochikoskaj
tlatoktsij youali kiiuintiaj.

Kochtok kanaktsij xinachtli
se tlatskintli xoxouik xochiisuatl.

IV

Virginal breasts,
buttons of dew.

Fragrance of the waning moon.

The ephemeral night is drunk
on your spring necklace.

The fragile seed sleeps,
a bouquet of green petals.

IV

Xochimantok kuauitl
monakayotia yolixtli mopaniko

Tepitsin. Tlatoktsij.

Ipan akueyojmej ueyatl,
kiuauasatsa ieltlapal apipialotl.

Tlamajtok tetl
axmolintli kiyeualoua.

V

Tree in flower
where life takes on flesh.

Fleeting. Brief.

The dragonfly's wings glance
the great water's waves.

Stone remains
surrounded by stillness.

VI

Youali kitsikauasjuia
kualantok mixtli.

Kimoyaua mestli tsakuxochipetlatl.

Ipan ajuechkali
tlitl neksayolimej teotekichiuaj.

Tlen yolistli patlantli
itech ueyatl xochitl tsopelik.

VI

Furious clouds
comb the night.

The moon spills her lily petals.

Bees of fire officiate
the house of dew.

Life's flight
in the flower's sweet sea.

VII

Ika xochikuikatl
tlali kikuanaua xinachtli.

Tlakatl iesso, miauatl.

Ixmijmijkayotl xiuitl kochistli,
temitok mestli ixouiyo.

Ika maitl ipan pamitl,
sintli kiijkuiloua xochikuikatl.

VII

With flowered song
the earth embraces the seed.

Man's blood, maize.

Dream is blinding greenery,
the full moon's leaves.

With hands in the furrow,
corn writes the poem.

TSOTSIL

CHIAPAS • MEXICO

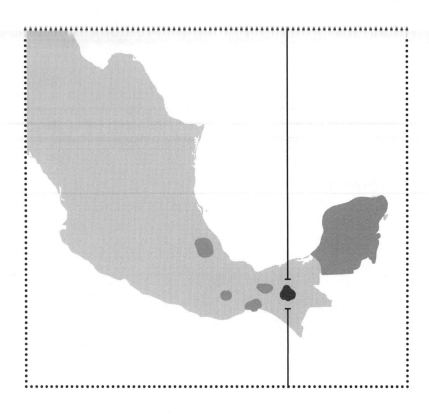

ENRIQUETA LUNEZ

TRANSLATED BY CLARE SULLIVAN

Though **Enriqueta Lunez** (b. 1981) is originally from San Juan Chamula, Chiapas, her first language was Spanish, not the indigenous Tsotsil. She learned the language of her parents and grandparents in grade school and started to write poetry at the age of twenty. She credits her paternal grandparents with her love of language and recalls how she used to hide in order to listen to adults speak.

To date Enriqueta has published three collections of poetry. She writes in the variant of Tsotsil spoken in Chamula.

Spoken in Eastern Central Mexico, Tsotsil is a Mayan language with six varying dialects, named after the different regions of Chiapas where they are spoken: Chamula, Zinacantán, San Andrés Larráinzar, Huixtán, Chenalhó, and Venustiano Carranza. These dialects have varying degrees of divergence and mutual intelligibility, and as a result some linguists consider them distinct languages. There are about 300,000 Tsotsil speakers in Mexico, and about 180,000 speakers of Chamula Tsotsil, which is the language of Enriqueta Lunez's poetry.

YAVU

Yo' k'uchal xich'na'el bu nak'al
ti vu'nejal t'ule
Ja'no'ox me xich' ch'unel,
ti yu'un oy t'ut' ti tae
te une, stak' ilel ti jaychop epal lo'il maxil
ta xcha' kuxanam ti' eile

LUNAR CALENDAR

To discover the distant lair
of the millenary hare
you must just believe
the moon has a beauty mark
and in it see a thousand legends
reborn on her lips.

VOBIL VAYICH

Te xi niknun
ja no'ox jna
ti te xi niknun
k'alal li julab
la kil mu chamen vinik
li bucho'o chamem
vu'un la jvektal kil

DELIRIUM

Trembling
I only remember
that I awoke
trembling
to see that body
the dead one
was I.

LA'MTABANEI

Li mut ta xk'ejin
li ts'i tax o'k
li moloch k'unk'un ta-x-och ta yut a vayich
ta jujun ak'ubal cha vaychintanaba' a lapoj ik'al k'uilettik
Cha julab
jeche cha vat a vo'onton
cha cha' vay
cha vaychinaj
li k'usi cha vaychinta ta na
ta xalbot smelol.

SIGN

A bird sings
a dog cries
the wary snake climbs into your dreams
and one day you dream dressed in black.
You will wake
don't worry yourself for nothing.
You sleep
and dream
today's dream
will give an answer.

Vo'ne xa tal, li chon mu xaspa sba ta ton
   li mute' muyuk xa ta smalaot
      ti muyuk xa chtukanan ta banomil li jinichetik
Vo'ne xa tal, li ta'l' maukxa xpatlajet ta'a mala'el
   li kuchom sarutetik mu xa snutsik a nak'obal
Vo'ne xa tal, ti ch'ay ta joltik k'uyelan tax i'kban li chamel
   ja ti li chamel
      ja xa no'ox, camen nichimal k'opetik

It's been so long already, that the serpent is not stone
    that the bird does not come to wait for you
        that ants don't pour from the earth.
It's been so long already, that the dog doesn't drag because
    you're gone
that cats in heat don't follow your dead shadow.
It's been so long already, we forgot the summons of death

    because death
    itself is metaphor muerta.

CHAMEL

Xvajbun
x ok'olet
sts'ijet
ta xjoch sba
li ts'i'
ta xokon
ech'
li chamele'

DEATH

Barks
wails
quiets down
drags itself
the dog
beside it
passed by
death.

La jti jbe' svayel kajvaltik
jutun sk'an o'lol ak'obal
sjelobil svayel
la jk ak lit'
vukub nichimal k'op
vukub a vokol
la jchapbe' jmul
skotol jmul
la jbuts'bc' sti ba.
La jti jbe' svayel kajvaltik
jutun sk'an o'lol ak'obal
li o'ra mux ech' no'ox yaluk
tilanuk vuk tos kantilaetik
li banomil la yuch' ch'ul pox
k'unk'un li yav ak'al la stu'm sba
li ts'ebal alai la sjoybi'nsba ta jbektal.
La jti jbe' svayel kajvaltik
jutun sk'an o'lol ak'obal
k'unk'un li o'ra
la sjoybin jk'op ta kambail.

I woke up God
around midnight
in exchange for his wakefulness
I offered
seven verses
seven pardons.
I confessed my sins
all my offenses
and kissed his forehead.
I woke up God
around midnight
and timeless time
consumed the seven colors
the earth drank holy moonshine
slowly the censer burned out
a dove became my flesh.
I woke up God
around midnight
and little by little time
turned my prayer to purest desire.

A VOKOLUK

Lis ch'ich'ele uch'bo
ch'ul banomil
li xchinabe' takintasvo'
a k'o joybijuk ta chubaj
k'usi oy ta yut xchu't ak'o k'au'k
k'ucha'al o xcham
li slekilale elk'ambo'
ich'bo ch'el lis kuxlejale'
ja no'ox, mu xa bak skelun
ma'uk me sta ta ilel
ti bu'un ta xkakbe' vokolale'

ENTREATY

Mother earth,
drink her blood
dry up her brains
so she goes crazy
rot her entrails
to make her die
rob her luck
and her innocence
only, do not let her look at me
so she won't know
that I'm the one who torments her.

Ta sakubel osil
li k'ak'ale'
ta smala li ants'e muts'ulto sat
ta sakubel osil x-joybij satik li vinitketik ta sk'elik chvə'ktal
 li k'ak'ale
ja ti ta sta'ik ta k'oponel jtotik sventa xnatij xkuxlejalike

Ja yo'rail yu'un jtotiketik

Ta anil o'lol k'ak'al
li kampanaetik ta xk'ejinik ta yut jk'ontonik
li jtotike' ta slokta sba ta nak'obal.

Ja yo'rail yu'un jtotiketik.
Ja yo'rail smalk'inelik ta pom.

Ta slajem li k'ak'al xchi'uk stekel k'ak'aletik
ko'ol te ta stsomsba' nichimetik xchi'uk li mal k'ak'ale
ta yolon k'ok' xa me xchi'uk ok'el ta x-och li ak'obale
te no'ox ta kos kos k'op ta xalbe sba'ik ta yan to k'ak'al

Já yo'rail y'un jtotiketik
Ja yo'rail smalk'inelik ta pom
Ja yo'rail kalal li j me'e ta sta ta k'oponel li jtotike'.

In the milky light of dawn
time proclaims
the presence of the sleeping woman
of men who look back to the first rays
of a prayer that stretches life.

They are the hours of saints.

In the brevity of noon
the song of bells resounds on the inside
the sun puts on its living raiment of shadows.

They are the hours of saints.
They are the hours of incense.

At the end of this and all days
horizon flowers glow their cloudy yellow
feasting the gentled whispers
with lights and lamentations.

They are the hours of saints.
They are the hours of incense.
They are the hours of my mother praying.

CH'UL ME MARUCH'

Ab'al la staik ta alel stekel sbi' li jch'ulmetike
ja mu'tix la yalik a bi'
Maruchal antsil
chi' n Maruchal ants
la sk'amboxuk bijil jolal, slekilal kuxlejal
Jun mu sikil li ak'obale'
li me' alak k'unk'un xcham
ti k'opetik xchi'uk pakolil, tas ta'ananik
ta na'el li me'el-moletik

HOLY WOMAN MARY

Without mentioning all virgins
they named you
Holy Mary woman
Holy Mary child
they begged you for protection, wisdom.
Our night is oh so cold
the poor hen's death drags on.
What sacrifice and words evoke
our ancestors' voice, terse and bright?

TA BA MUKINAL

Ta ba mukinal mu a'ybaj chkux jch'ulel.

Ta ba mukinal
yaxal k'anal nichimetik
ta sk'i ti jvokolajel ch'ulelale.

Ta ba mukinal,
xnoplajet xojobal k'ok' ta spat yo'on yo' k'uchal mu xtup' sakubel
    osil.

Ta ba mukinal
nich pox
ya'lel kuxlejal
xch'olet yalel ta nuk'iletik.

Ta ba mukinal,
balumilal k'abal
chk'ejin xchi'uk osil k'ak'al.

Ta ba mukinal,
jujun k'in Santo
ti sbi ch'ulelaletike
ta xich'ik tael ta na'el, ta xich'ik nak'el

OVER THE GRAVE

My anxious soul rests over the grave.

Green and yellow flowers
clothe my mourning soul
over the grave.

The lights dissolve over the grave,
hope not to be extinguished by the dawn.

Nich pox
extract of life
pours down throats
over the grave.

Earthly hands
sing with the season
over the grave.

Every All Saints Day
the names of all souls
are remembered and kept
over the grave.

CH'UL BANOMIL

Yo k'uchal mu kunil son
li ba' banomil chmiknun
yu'un skoj k'opetik xchi'uk ch'ul vayichiletik.

SACRED LAND

And the earth trembled at the sound
of a tender touch
buzzing helpless words and sacred dreams.

Ta jmui'mtas ta pom lia be'ktal ta kopale
taj jsaku'mtas li xtal a be'e
ta jnojesot ta ts'ibetik k'ejimol
ta jmallaol ta xunel pajn'mtaolil pox
Ta k'un k'un chkal li k'usi mu xa jna' yo' mu xa va'ie
ta jaxulan ta kok li k'usi muk'bu na'bile
k'anbilot xapas aba'
k'alal cha vak'bon li jamal slajebal a vik'e.

I bless your smooth skin with incense
light up your next destination
satisfy the endless notes of your soul
pour subtle infusions upon you.
I whisper secret spells that you don't hear
caress strange roots with my feet
you are tame and good-hearted
as you bestow on me your final naked exhalation.

JPETS' JTE'

Te ta sat jna ta xkil jpets' te'
ti yabilal mu jna'
Manuchuk me xotkinbil yu'un ti ik'e.
Ja' jech jk'anok o:
Oy xchamel ta sjelubtas ta yol xnich'on,
sbek'tal silambil yu'un sik
xchi'uk ti stoyubbail alak' sba o xchi'uke.

Bak'intike ta jxi' ti svokol ok'ele,
sk'a'emal chamel te nochol oe
xchi'uk ti k'usi vokolil ta xak
me oy jech xnijbuje
Toj alak' sba sna'oj
ja' ta xak' ta ilel ti jun yutsil kuxlejale.

MY TREE

From the window I can see a tree
whose age I don't remember.
And though the wind has warped it
I love it still:
With the sickness it inherits,
with its body broken down by winter
and with the pride that gives it beauty.

At times I fear its anguished cry,
the leprosy that clings to it
the damage that could happen
if it bowed in two.
Conscious of its grace
it shows us the divine bloom of the living.

VU'UN LI' OYUNKUTIKE

Mu'yuk bu chamemunkutik ta yech'emal kuxlejal
mu yu'unuk chitajinkutik ta yak'el jbakutik ta ilel.
Vu'unkutik,
k'ux osil k'ak'al ta spat ti yoytolal k'ak'aletike,
ta yuninal mu'yuk jamen satil ta k'u sjalil mu'yuk ch'akbil ta ilel.

Manchuk me ech'em ta o'lol yoxbok'al jme'tik u
yiloj ti la kichkutik mukele:
Ta jaylajunbok' jtotik yiloj yich ch'ayel ya o'nale.
Ja' no'ox yu'un,
mu baluk ta jun u.
Oy van yik'al,
me jeche,
vo'vinik xcha' bok'al jtotik to xtok
ti boch'o chil chch'ay ti jol ko'ontone
xchi'uk ta xyik t'anal chlaj ti jbektale.

K'alal me laj ti k'usi t'abal ta jol o'ntonale,
mu xa boch'o ta snuts ti k'usi te nak'al
te van bak'in, te van bu',
k'ejel ta jkuxlejal.

I AM THOSE WE ARE HERE

We are not dead in the past
nor do we play at an appearance in this world.
We are,
and it weighs upon the back of calendars,
upon the tender ignorance of unrecorded time.

In spite of a thousand moons
that have witnessed our burial:
A thousand suns witnessed our forgetting.
Still,
one moon is not enough.
There will
most likely be
five hundred more suns
to watch my memory erase
and my naked body die.

When the remembrance fizzles
no one will manage to pursue the secrets
sheltered in my being
somewhere, at some time.

SVENTA MUK'TOTIL

Sjayibal k'ak'al
laka'i k'opoj li jmuk'totc
lok' ta ye jech
jun muk'u jecj lo'il a'yej

K'alal kerem to'oxe
tu yut li muk'tik pinkaetike
yil la ital jun vinik
K'alal xchap ti slo'ile
vul ta jol ta jsat,
kil la va'al ta sts'el muk'tot
li jch'ultokik Xun
ta jole la ikil ti xojobale, li yanjelale,

Ko'ol chak nen ta nom
ikil kejel.
Ya'i jchikin li sk'optake, li k'usi chale

Li k'usi chale, naka sventa vinajel
yu'un ch'abal ti vo'e
jech un tsk'an ti ch'ul vo' ta vinajele
ti ak'u bajuk ta takin banomil
bajlajetuk ti ya'lel nabe, bajlajetuk la yilel.

Tal no'ox ti mantal ta anile
xk'echlajet ti yok vo' ta jlikelbane
ch'ay me ti takin banomil

Ja' jech, ta jnop ta jol un:

FOR GRANDPA

A few days ago
I heard my grandpa speak
and from his mouth came forth
an incredible tale.

When he was young
out on the great estates
he saw the apparition of a man.
Listening to his words transformed in tale
I imagined myself
see St. John stand
before my grandpa
my fantasy thought it saw the bolts, heard the thunder.

And like a far off mirage
I saw him prostrate.
My ears heard his words, his pleas.

His pleas were only for the sky
it had not rained.
He asked the keeper of the sky
ceaselessly to let a few drops fall
from the sea to this infertile land,
a sea that sometimes seems to
fall.

The answer did not wait
and the waves swept over
the desert at that moment.

And till today I ask myself:

Bats'i k'uxi ya'el
k'uxi jech ak'bil o ti jmol tote,
Yu'un lek tsakbil ti ye sti'e.
Li avie, mujna, yu'un ja' jech chkil
li vini le'e
yu'un, molib xa un.

What divine messenger
gave grandpa grace
gave his words strength
even though today my eyes
see him changed
into an old man.

ISTHMUS ZAPOTEC

OAXACA • MEXICO

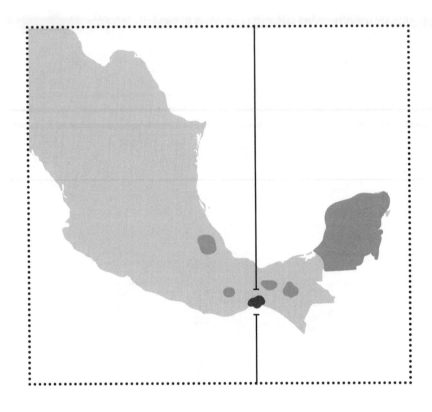

VÍCTOR TERÁN

TRANSLATED BY DAVID SHOOK

Víctor Terán was born in Juchitán de Zaragoza in 1958, and his work has been published extensively in magazines and anthologies throughout Mexico. His books of poetry include *Sica ti Gubidxa Cubi* [*Like a New Sun*] and *Ca Guichi Xtí' Guendaranaxhii* [*The Spines of Love*]. Terán works as a media education teacher at the secondary level on the Oaxacan Isthmus. His work has appeared in *Oxford Review, PN Review Poetry, World Literature Today,* and many other magazines. A chapbook of his translations is available from the Poetry Translation Centre in London, produced for his tour of the UK in 2010. In addition to his work as poet and teacher, Terán is a translator into Isthmus Zapotec, having translated poets from Wordsworth to Bukowski. His work has been nominated for a Pushcart Prize and broadcast on BBC4. In 2014, Restless Books published his trilingual selected poetry as *The Spines of Love.*

Isthmus Zapotec is an indigenous Mexican language from the Otomanguean family. The last formal census, in 2000, suggests that there are 75,000 to 100,000 speakers of the Isthmus dialect, which is one of up to 40 mutually unintelligible dialects of the language. Zapotec is a Verb-Subject-Object language with heavy affixing and clitics. It is a tonal language that employs the frequent use of glottal stops, which characterize the rhythms of its poetry. Isthmus Zapotec's contemporary literature dates back almost 200 years, making it one of the most developed and vigorous contemporary indigenous literary traditions in Mexico.

BIETE BI

Biete bi.
Lu neza gui'chi' ne bacuela
nanda saaca' ne xiana.
Ruguubeedxe' ca yoo,
ridopa cuuxhu' bi'cu'.
Daabi ti xiixa
bicuininá' huadxí ri':
ti guichi guluxu,
ti guiiba' tini.

Nuu tu laa
gudu'ba' xhaata' gueza guibá',
bisaana ni naté, nagu'xhu'.
Xaguete' ri' guiruti'
nibeezá xpandá',
guirá' zeguyoo ra lidxi
cugaba' xquenda zí'.

Caxidxi zinña,
laaca tuuxa biaanatá'
gudxite xcunaa laa.

Yanadxí guirá'
bietenala'dxi' ladeñee,
málasi gunna binni
nuu guendaruseegu' ra lidxi.

Tu laa nanna
xiñee cazaaca' huadxí ri',
xiñee nisi nuaa'
gudxiga' yaana' xii
bixé' cundubi rarí'.

THE NORTH WIND WHIPS

The north wind whips through,
in the streets papers and leaves
are chased with resentment.
Houses moan,
dogs curl into balls.
There is something in the afternoon's finger,
a catfish spine,
a rusty nail.

Someone unthinkingly
smoked cigarettes in heaven,
left it overcast, listless.
Here, at ground level, no one could
take their shadow for a walk,
sheltered in their houses, people
are surprised to discover their misery.

Someone didn't show,
their host was insulted.
Today the world
agreed to open her thighs,
suddenly the village comprehends
that it is sometimes necessary to close their doors.

Who can divine
why I meditate on this afternoon?
Why is it birthed in me
to knife the heart
of whoever uncovered the mouth
of the now whipping wind,
to jam corncobs in the nose
of the ghost that pants outside?

Cuxidxi ca yaga,
riaba riásaca'
cuxidxica' naa
runi biaanala'ya'.

Latané naa nagasi
guirá' manihuiini' ruunda'
guidxélatu lu yaga,
ti gabe' laatu
pa naye'que' guichalaga binidxaba'.

The trees roar with laughter,
they split their sides,
they celebrate
that you haven't arrived at your appointment.

Now bring me
the birds
that you find in the trees,
so I can tell them
if the devil's eyelashes are curled.

YUDÉ CUYAA

Yudé cuyaa galaabato' ná' tapa neza.
Ca yaga nagá' caguíteca' tu jmá naguudxi deche.
Ladxiduá' nexhegaa lu luuna' cabeza lii, bezaluá' zuba,
rinaaze' bi guichaíque, zuba, cugaba' panda bihui
culaa xii ti xcuidi zubaxuuna'.

Laga lii ya', xi cayuni ndou' nagasi.
Nannu' xiinga guendaribeza ti gunaa
gueeda guxhídxiná'
lu gande iza xtí' ti badunguiiu la?

Yudé cuyaa galaabato' bizaluá'.
Ti mani' canareeguite ndaani' ca nezarini xtinne'.
Gunaa bazeendu', xi binidxaba' cayu'nu' qui gueedu'.
Ma' bigaba' birá bicuininá' gubidxa,
bi yooxho' ma' bigani lu neza, bidxaga ruaa,
cachuundu', ma' nacahui guibá',
ndaaninaya' nexheguundu' guguhuiini'
guleza lii.

134

WHIRLWIND

The dust dances in the middle of the path.
The leafy trees compete to make the most elegant curtsies.
My heart stretched across the bed, waiting for you. Quiet eyes,
the air tangles your hair, quiet, the pigs make known
that they attack the boy squatting to do his business.

And you, what would you be doing in this instant?
Do you, by chance, know what it is to wait for a woman
who comes to touch
the twenty waiting years of a man?

The dust dances in the eclipse of my eyes.
A chestnut fizzes through the paths of my blood.
Perverse woman, where the hell are you, what the hell are you
    doing?
I've already counted each of the sun's fingers,
the wind's gust quit exciting the street, silenced by fatigue.
It is twilight, the sky is filled with shadows,
in my hands it lies dying,
the turtledove that dreamed of cooing you to sleep.

NEEGUE' CA

Neegue' ca nga
sica ti xcuidi
nacu ti neza lari cubi
xquendaranaxhiee'.

Neegue' ca nga
rilué' xquiibalé yu'du'
ze' ne zeeda
cabidxi yeche' mixa'.

Yanna nuaa'
sica ti binidxaapa' bida'na'
ne qui nuxooñenécabe laa,
sica ti gubidxa bidé xiaga
ni gatigá rindisa bi
          rucheeche laa.

JUST YESTERDAY

Just yesterday
my love was
like a kid breaking in
the year's new clothes.

Just yesterday
I was a bell
joyfully coming and going
announcing mass.

Now I am
like the virgin bride whose lover
refused consummation,
like a sun finished burning
whose ash
        is scattered by the wind.

QUI ZUNIHUARÁLU NAA

Qui zunihuarálu' naa.
Qui zaguza dlou' xquendanabane'.
Naro'ba' yu'du' biaani' bisananelu' naa,
nanaadxi' ne nayeche'.

Xadxípe' bisindá'naxhilu' bi stinne',
xadxípe' guleezalu' naa lade ca za
ne xidxaa guidiládilu'.

Racaditi ru' ca naya' guietenala'dxica'
beelaxiaa dxitaxa'nalu'.
Ricaala'dxiru' guidiruaa'
runi guiropa' rii dxiñabizu xi'dxu'.

Paraa chiguniná guendarietenala'dxi' naa ya'.
Paraa, neca zelu', gácananaladxe' lii ya'.
Ti nisadó' benda riaquibiaani' bisananelu' naa,
ti nisadó' benda caguite yeche'.

YOU WILL NOT MANAGE TO HURT ME

You will not manage to hurt me.
You will not break my existence.
The cathedral of light that you left me is immense,
warm and joyful.

You scented my existence for a long time.
You introduced me to paradise
with your lukewarm and naked body.

My hands still shake at the memory
of your fleshy ass.
My lips still tremble
when I remember the taste of your nipples.

With these memories, how can I feel hurt?
Though you left me, how can I abhor you?
You left me with an ocean of dazzling fish,
an ocean of incessant fish.

GUIDÚBILU' RUNEBIA'YA'

Guidúbilu' runebia'ya',
guidúbiluaca peou'.
Pa ñácalu' ti guidxi
ratiicasi ninabadiidxa' cabe náa
naa nulué' pa neza riaana ní.
Riuuládxepea' guidúbilu',
riuuladxe' guuya' guiní'lu', guxídxilu',
guzeque yannilu'. Dxiña yaga guiropa' dani
zuguaa ndí' xtilu', ra guyaa' dxiqué
rigucaa' ruaa bidó'. Ñacaladxe' rua'
ñuá' ne niree ndaani' guixhidó' xtilu',
ni guya' dxiiña' guiluxe guendanabani ndaani'.
Biza'naadxi' bido' guzana lii, qui gápalu'
ra guidiiñeyulu'. Binnindxó' nga naa
ti bibane' lii, guca' lii. Yanna ma cadi naa
ridxiiche' gudxigueta lú ca nguiiu ra zedi'dilu',
ma cadi naa racalugua' cueelu' lari.
Ti bidxiña lubí nga lii, ti balaaga' guie'
ziguite yeche' lu guiigu' ti siadó'.

Gabati' lii nou' qui ñunebia'ya', nou'
qui ñuuladxe'. Pa ñándasi ñácarua'
biaani' ruxheleruaa ruuya' ca nduni
yuxido' quichi' beelaxa'nalu'. Pa ñándasi
nibeza rua'
        ndaani' guidxi sicarú
                ni nácalu'.

I KNOW YOUR BODY

I know your body,
entirely I know you.
If you were a city
I could give perfect directions
to wherever they asked me.
I like all of your body,
I like to see you talk, laugh,
move your head. Your two well-rounded hills
are the honey of bees, where my lips celebrate to the gods.
I would have liked to continue storming your forest,
lodgings made deliberately for a nice death.
You were created with love,
your body is worthy of praise. What an honor to have lived,
to have been. I am no longer bothered
when men turn to look at you,
I am no longer impatient when you undress.
You are a stag in the air. A raft of flowers
that snakes across the river by morning.

There is no part of your body that I do not know, there is no
part that I do not like. I want to keep being
the light stunned at the look of your white
roundness of flesh. I want to keep
living
　　　in the beautiful city
　　　　　　that you are.

LÁ LU'

Ridxí ne huaxhinni, lá lu'.
Siadó', huadxí, lu gueela'
nisi lá lu' riree xieque
ndaani' bichuga íque'
sica tuuxa zeguyoo
runi biniti guendabiaani',
nisi lá lu' riree chuuchi
lu ludxe'
sica benda ndaani' ná'
ti guuze'.

Guindisa' ti gui'chi', lá lu',
cuaque' ti xiixa, lá lu'.
Gabati' nalu' nuaa'
cadi daabi guichi lá lu'
íque bicuini naya',
ne ratiicasi zedide'
málasi gó la'na'
guendarietenala'dxi' lú lu'
ñee xquendanabane'.

Ma yanna nga nabaana
ne huidxe mápeca saa guidxi.
Zándaca ridxí zaxhaca la'dxi'
sá' nanda huaxhinni.
Zándaca naa guibane' ti dxi
ne guirá' ca yaya xtí' xquendagute',
zapa ruá' ti nisadó' guendaricaala'dxi'
ndaani' ladxiduá' guzeete' lá lu',
zápa' rua' neca xtuudxi huiini' bi
guzayaniá' ti dxumisú birixhiaa
gusitenala'dxi' lii guendaranaxhii stinne'
sica rusietenala'dxi' laanu ne xquendayaya
dxi ma zeedadxiña xhí nisaguié.

142

YOUR NAME

Day and night, your name.
In the morning, the afternoon, at dusk
only your name spins
through my head
like a man straight-jacketed
for having lost his mind;
only your name slips
over my tongue
like a fish between the hands
of a fisherman.

I lift a paper, your name.
I put something away, your name.
There is nowhere I go
that I do not have the thorn of your name
nailed to the tip of my finger
and no matter where I go,
the memory of your face silently bites
the leg of my existence.

It is time for Lent
and May's festival is near.
Perhaps the day is fed up
with chasing the night.
Maybe one day I'll wake up
to the scandal of my death;
despite it all I'll have an ocean of sighs
in my soul, to whisper your name;
I'll undoubtedly have one last breath
capable of filling a basket with winged ants
that will proclaim the love I have,
like the commotion that announces
coming rains.

HUADXÍ QUE ZIYABA

Biluuza ti ridxi
ndaani' yánilu',
ti ridxi naxiñá'
guizá' dxichi
bitubi lu luuna'.

Huadxí que ziyaba,
gunna ni naa
ti lu neza binadia'ga' zixidxi
chuppa guidibo'co' nayeche'.

Bindaate' xpié'
cue'diágalu'
laga ca naya' naazedxiichi',
ziyuí' xtípaca', ziguxooñe' naca',
ziyabaneca' naa guidxilayú.

Huadxí que ziyaazi',
gunna' dxindxe' piá'
ti biiya' cayábayati
ca lágalu'.

THE AFTERNOON FELL

From your throat
a broken cry,
a red cry
entirely whole
rolled on the bed.

The afternoon fell,
I knew
because of the two brave shoes
that echoed through the street.

I spilled my breath
over your shoulders,
while my vigorous and headstrong hands
grew weak, lowering your body
until it was one with me on the floor.

The afternoon was sinking in,
I knew it fully
by the slow movement
of your eyelids.

TOBI SI

Tobi si randa riaba
ra lidxi guendarluuxtubi.
Yu'du' nabé' dxita
ra rigué' nisa
ca ladxidó' cayati.
Yu'du' naguchi te
zuxalendaga
dxi ne gueela'.

JUST ONE

Loneliness' house
can lodge just one.
Fair temple
where hearts at odds
arrive to rest.
Yellow sanctuary
wide open
by day and by night.

DXUCA'

icaa Víctor Yodo

Xiñee zinetu
dxuca',
badunguiiu guichi zundí'
stiidxa'
ribana la'dxi'
Guidxiguie' stinne'.

Dxuca',
xi bi'nibe laatu?
Bixhatañeebe
yanni binnilídxitu la?
Bitúxhube xpi'cube
luguiá' bacaandaguie'
stitu la?

Dxuca',
lagabi naa,
cadi góyaatu diidxa'
redandá
lu lúdxitu.

Dxuca',
la guxhele ruaa.

SOLDIERS

for Víctor Yodo

Why,
soldiers,
did you kidnap
a man whose word is as true
as a thorn,
who yearns for
my flowered Juchitan?

Soldiers,
what grievance did he commit against you?
Did he stomp
on your family's necks?
Did he sic his dogs on
your
flowered dreams?

Soldiers,
tell me,
don't bite the words
that come
to your tongues.

Soldiers,
open your mouths.

BEEU

Beuu. Beeu quichi' sicarú
nica biaani' bizalú ti xí'
gudiñelaga ti lempa ndaani' gui'xhi'.

Beeu bilumbu' riga ca bé.
Beeu ndaani' ti gunaa nacaxiiñi'.
Beeu qui gapa guendabiaani'
sica ti bidxadxa nisa.

Beeu dxita gudi'di' xhí.
Beeu gulabere' mboolo' güí lu yaga:
bisiga'de' naa tindaa xquendanayéchelu'
gusigaanda' xquedanabani xquidxe'.

Beeu bidaaniquichi'
biaa íque ti xunaxi binnizá:
bisiga'de' naa ca bacuzaguí ladxido'lo'
guzaani' neza sá' ca xpinne'.

Beeu guizá', beeu dxa'tipa.
Beeu cuxidxisá
ne cagapaxa'na'.

MOON

Moon. Sweet white moon
like the gleam in the eye of an unlucky hunter
who chases a rabbit across the mountain.

Emptied and moldy cachimbo shell moon.
Pregnant belly moon.
Delirious moon
like a colander that dreams of overflowing with water.

Deformed egg moon.
Ripe rubber-fruit moon:
give me a slice of your joy
to refresh life in my town.

Ceremonial huipil moon
that adorns the Zapotec's head:
give me the fireflies that live in your heart
to light my people's paths.

Intact moon, full moon.
Moon happy to die laughing
slapping its ass.

_____

A *huipil* is a traditional blouse commonly worn by indigenous Mexican
women.

HUANDÍ'

Gusiga'de' Pedro Salinas (1891–1951)

Huandí'.
Biaana bi naxhi
xtí' guidiládilu' ndaani' yoo
ra rireechuuchi batañee
xquendabiaani' ladxiduá'.
Riasacaanda' xpisi xho' ca xi'dxu'
reedagucuaani' guendareedasilú xtí' ca naya'.
Nabana' ruuna' íqueyoo lidxe' lalu'.
Riaadxa' xidxaa xtilu' gusigaanda'
guendarigani cayuni ridxi rarí':

Bandaa ne yayayoo,
berendxinga ne guidiribeela.

Tu bidó' bizá' lii
qui nucaa tindaa ladxidó'lo'.
Ne xiñee pa nannu' zielu'
qui nucoou maniá' ñee xquendaranaxhiee'.
Cadi huaxa nanaladxe' lii.
Cadi huaxa cuchaya' gasti' lulu'.
Ni riuuba' naa nagasi nga
rabe' qui ñuu dxi ñuuba' naa xiixa.
Ne yanna nuaa' rarí'
ndaani' yoo yooxho' bi'ya'
gubidxa ne guiropa' beeu sicarú xtilu',
nuaa' canieniá' bandá' xtinne',
yaca yaca gugaanda' laa lu yaga,
yaca yaca gugaanda naa.

Xiné bicaalu' xiguidxa' guendanabani xtinne'.
Xi guichi quibaniá' ladxiduá' reza cuxhii rini.

IT'S TRUE

For Pedro Salinas (1891–1951)

It's true.
Your skin's scent remains in this room
where the feet of every reason
my heart births slip.
Your breasts' scent's muse
lingers to remind my hands of their history.
The ceiling mournfully babbles your name.
The silence that scandalizes my house
is not refreshed by your missing warmth.

Termite and cobwebs.
Crickets and bats.

Which of the gods gave you life
with that heart of stone?
And why if what we had was impossible
did you not shackle my love's feet?
But I don't hate you.
But I don't fault you at all.
What most hurts me now is admitting
you hurt me.
Look at me now
in this old house that knew
your sun and your two beautiful moons,
look at me talking to my shadow,
sometimes it occurs to me to strangle it,
sometimes it tries to hang me.

Tell me. What did you do to fray the string that keeps me alive?
What spine can I sew my heart back together with, before
    bleeding out?

BIU'DXU'

1

Biu'dxu' yanna, gubidxa,
gutiyaa ne guendasicarú xtilu'.
Ladxiduá' ma' qui zadidilaaga' gucueeza ca guie
rundaa guendanabani luguialu',
bizaluá' ma' qui zacalugu'
gu'ya' gandagaa guendanabana'
ca laga sicarú lu'.
Bitoope yanna, guie'tiiqui'
ne guyé yedaabi gabiá.

2

Gugabi binidxaba' lii
ti bidxí nayaa, guizá' dxichi.
Guzu'nda' Diuxi neza zelu'
guirá' ca xiana huadii guidxilayú laa.
Guibi'xhu' batañeelu',
ne ca nalu' guiaya xtubi
dxi gacala'dxu' guinábalu' guibá'
gusiaanda' ca yuuba' bisaananelu' naa.
Guixele' guidxilayú ra guzuguaalu',
gabi binidxaba' lii.

ROT

1

Rot now, sun,
die, without relief, with your beauty.
My heart will not be the shield that
blocks the stones life throws at you.
My eyes will no longer be troubled
when they see sadness
hang from your beautiful eyelashes.
Fade now, prized flower,
and beat it—plunge into hell.

2

May the devil force you
to swallow a prickly pear, green and whole.
May God throw all the rage
that the world has directed at him across your path.
May your feet atrophy
and your hands turn to dust
when you try to beg forgiveness from the skies
for the suffering you left me.
May the earth open up wherever you pause
and may the devil throw you into the abyss.

NUZAYA' LII

Ñetenala'dxe' guidiruaalu'
sica rietenala'dxe' padxí
ne paraa binebia'ya' lii.

Ñetenala'dxe' guendaruyadxí stilu'
sica xa bixidu' nirudó' bidiilu' naa,
sica xho' guiropa' stagabe'ñe' mudu
bisindá' naxhi nelu' guidiruaa'.

Ñannapia' nidxela' lii
ndaani' bizaluá' de'gu'
sícape' ridxela' ra lídxilu'
neca ma' naxudxe'.

Niziidepia' nuzaya' lii,
nuzayadxiiña' piá' lii,
íque si ná' ladxiduá',
sica ruzá' manihuiini' lidxi,
sica riá' ti bidó'.

IF I KNEW HOW TO SCULPT YOU

If I could remember your lips
as I remember the day
and place where we met.

If I could remember your gaze
like the first kiss that you gave me,
like the scent of your two budding water lilies
that perfumed my lips.

If I knew how to find you
with my eyes closed
like I find your house
even beneath the veil of alcohol.

If I knew how to sculpt you,
I would patiently give you form
with the tips of my soul's fingers,
like the birds weave their nests,
like a God is built.

BIBANENIÁ' LALU'

Bibaneniá' lalu' naga' ndaani' yanne'.
Pa nlnf' ca naya' nl gunlé'xcaanda'
ñuuyapiá' nusabalú diuxi.
Bandaa cayuni xhiiña' lu gueela'
sica ti gubaana' biziidichaahui'.
Ne lu bi za'bi' guendaruyadxí bana' xtinne'
naaze nanda guidiruaa.

Gasti' nou' qui runebia'ya' ndaani' yoo ra nuaa'
ne zacá ladxiduá' cayacaditi
sica ti xcuidi guladxi bi'cu'.
Rahuayaa bicuininá' xquendabiaane'
ti guibani chaahui'.
Laga ti gayuaa bigose buubu
ziyásanene lu layú ladxiduá'.

Ze'gu' lu beeu huaxhinni.
Naaze guppa larigueela' yaase' xtí' guibá'.
Pa ñanna' caniéxcaanda' qui nundaa' ca nalu',
pa ñanna' zabane' niguiidxedxiiche' lii ti que ñelu'.
Rigui'ba' ti yuuba' ra yanne'
ne ricaa runi xtí' ladxiduá'.

Paraa nda' nuu ca luyaande sicarú lu' ya',
paraa nda' ca guidiruaalu'.
Biaanaru' xiixa xtinne'
ndaani' ladxidó'lo' la?
Huandí' nga ma' biaanda' lii
ni gúcanu la?

Bibaneneá' lalu' naga' ndaani' yanne'.

I WOKE WITH YOUR NAME

I woke with your name stuck in my throat.
If my hands would say what I dreamed last night
I am certain that God would lower his gaze.
The termite labors at night
like an experienced thief.
And my languid face hangs in the air
with a light trembling of lips.

Nothing exists in this house that I do not know
but even so my heart shakes
like a child chased by a dog.
I bite the feet of my understanding
to wake it from its stupor.
Meanwhile a flock of rooks
lifts into flight, slowly,
from the empty field of my soul.

It's night and the moon is covered.
The humidity suffocates the black sheet of the sky.
If I had known I was dreaming
I would not have let go of your hands.
If I had known I was dreaming
I would have hugged you tightly
so you wouldn't leave.
A pain rises up my throat
and clenches my heart.

In what place do your large, beautiful eyes walk about,
in what place your lips?
Does anything of mine still
exist within your heart?
Is it true that you will forget
all that we were?

I woke with your name stuck in my throat.

BISEEGULU'

Biseegulu' ra lídxilu',
hixa'hu' yaga ladxiduá'
Zuuya' lii guixí' la?
Nisi le xtidxe'
guxidxi biluuza ñee lu bi
xa'na' gueela' cahui.
Gurié' deche li'dxu',
guduba' ti gueza.
Rabe' pa guiasa' chaa',
guixí' neca gate'
ra nuulu' ma' qui zabigueta'.
Bixhidxenaya' ra li'dxu' nagueenda,
bixhidxenaya' nadipa'.
Biduxhu chupa bi'cu'
ne huaxhinni
birendachaahui' xhabagueela'.
Gunié' lalu'.
Ne ti ridxi yati
gunié lalu',
gudxe' lii:
ma' qui zabigueta',
gulee lú
bicueeza naa.
Gasti',
ti la'pa' gue'tu'
naca ladxiduá' yanna,
ne chii beendagubizi
ca bicuininaya'.

160

YOU CLOSED

You closed the door,
sealing off my heart.
Will I see you tomorrow?
My lonely voice
was heard staggering through the air
beneath the dark night.
I sat next to your house
and smoked a cigarette.
I swore that if I left without seeing you
even though the pain would undo me
I would not return.
I hastily knocked on the door.
I hopelessly knocked.
Two dogs barked
and the night rolled over
beneath her sheets.
I said your name,
in my broken voice,
I said your name.
Come out to stop me.
I told you.
'Cause if I leave I'll never come back.
Nothing,
my heart is now
a mournful crown,
my fingers are
ten poisonous snakes.

BIXIDU'

Ti dxumi benda.
Chupa guixhe niza
Chonna bixidu'.
Bindaate', gudiibi.
Bichuxhi, guxuuba'.
Dané naa ne zaa guti.

KISSES

A basket of fish.
Two nets full of corncobs.
Three kisses.
Upturn it, clean them.
Husk them, strip off their kernels.
Give them to me, then you can die.

CO'

¡Tapa domi' bi
ne ti xiga nisa!

Nuu ti badunguiiu cayati
ndaani' guidxi Xavizende
lu beeu cha'hui'.

Co', co':
¡Ti yagalé
ne chupa xiga
     nisadxu'ni'!

NO

Fifty cents of air
and a pitcher of water!

A man suffers
in Juchitan
during prosperous times.

No, no:
A guitar
and two pitchers
    of mezcal!

YANADXÍ LA? RABE'

Yanadxí la? rabe'
qui zuzeete' lii,
qui zahuayaa bixuganaya'
ma' nuaa' cayetenala'dxe' lii.
Ziasa' ziaa' dxiiña',
zune' naa nahuati
pa gasti' ni gune'.
Zacaa' zugaba' ngu'xhi' lubí,
pa caa zucaala'dxe' guiene'
xiñee birí ma ze' ne ma zeeda
ne qui rati runi guendaranaxhii.
Zacaa' zuxhiee' bayu' xtinne'
pa nandá', zaxubenaya' lade',
diaga', lua' pa nananda.
Zacaa' zuchayaxhinne' lubí, layú,
pacaa zacaa' ti yaga ne ma ziaa',
ma ziaa' ziguzaa' laa guidxilayú,
tílasi ti dxi guedaguuyu' duuba' ca,
sa' nandu' ní
ne gueedaguidxaaganu xti bieque,
quiidxidxiichinu tobi
ne ganaxhiinu
sícaca gunaxhiinu
dxi xa dxi gúcanu tóbisi.

TODAY I ASPIRE

Today I aspire
not to mention you,
I will not bite my nails
thinking of you.
I will go to work,
I will become a senseless babbler
if I have nothing to do.
I will dedicate myself to counting the buzzards in the sky,
or else I will set out to understand
why ants come and go
and never suffer for love.
I'll wring my handkerchief
if it is hot, I will rub my arms together,
my ears, my face if it is cold.
I will spit upwards, downwards,
or else I will take a stick and I will go,
I'll go out and I'll furrow the earth,
hoping that one day you'll recognize the scratch
and follow it
and we will find each other again
to embrace anew,
to adore each other
as in that time
when we were one single person.

YUCATEC MAYA

CAMPECHE • MEXICO

BRICEIDA CUEVAS COB

TRANSLATED BY JONATHAN HARRINGTON

Briceida Cuevas Cob (b. 1969) is a Mayan poet from Tepakán, Campeche, Mexico. She has published several poetry books, including *U yok'ol awat peek'* [*The Dog's Moan*], *Je' bix k'iin* [*Like The Sun*], *Ti' u billil in nook'* [*From the Hem of My Dress*]. Her poems have been translated into French, Dutch, English, and Italian. She is a founding member of the Mexican Steering Committee of Writers of Indigenous Languages.

Yucatec Maya is spoken among the indigenous people of the Yucatán Peninsula of Mexico and northern Belize. The language has about 800,000 speakers today, in the Mexican states of Yucatán, some parts of Campeche, where Cuevas Cob is from, Tabasco, Chiapas, and Quintana Roo, and an additional 6,000 speakers in Belize.

Yucatec Maya is a two-tone language. The language makes use of ejective consonants, which are written using an apostrophe to distinguish them from plain consonants. Yucatec Maya had a written script that predates the colonial presence in the region, but is now written in Latin script, introduced during the Spanish conquest of the Yucatán that began in the early 16th century.

P'ÚUL

Táan u jaats' k'iin.
Tu meentik u chooj in k'ilkab tu táan in pool.
Táan u báaytiken u ki' síisil x-noj ch'e'en.
P'úule' ti' yaan tin wiknale',
in weet taal,
táan u che'ej tin wetel.
Kex uk'aje', tats' k'iin tu che'ej.
Táan in ki' jóojol chàachik.
Tin ki' sáaptik u báaxal kaanil suun,
ku ki' kopkuba tin wook.
Tu paach suun táan u taal u ch'óoyil ja'.
Tin ts'áik ja' u yuk' p'úul.
Táan u chan k'aay tu xúuchik ja'.
U k'aaye' u pekpekxiik' juntúul box k'a'aw ki'imak u yóol.
Luk' u yuk'ajil p'uul.
Tin ki' lóochaj,
tin méek'aj,
kex seten ko'.
Táan u chajlik in nak' yéetel u xikin,
bey xan u chajlik in ch'ala'atel.
Táan u ki' túubik in k'a'.
Táan xan u taal u joyja'atik lu'um utia'al in xíimbal.
Ma' tu jéets'el u ko'i'.
Mix tu jéets'el u chajlik in nak' yéetel u xikin.
¿Ma' wáaj táan u yilik
in machmaj ch'óoy yéetel in ts'íik k'a',
yéetel xan in páajkalmaj suun?
¿Ma' wa táan u tuklik
Je' bix u meentik in che'eej,
bey xan u bin u meentik in jáalk'abtik ka' in pa'e'?
Mix ba'al ku yilik,
mix ba'al ku tuklik,
chen leep'el u yóol u meent in che'ej.
Mix ba'al kin wilik,
mix ba'al kin tuklik,
chen táan in bin in jajache'ej yéetel p'úul.

THE STONE JUG

The sun strikes,
making my forehead sweat.
I draw near to the great well's freshness.
The stone jug is with me,
my strolling companion,
smiling at me.
It laughs all the time, even when it is thirsty.
I handle it with pleasure.
I struggle with the rope, a toy serpent,
rolled up at my feet.
With it I lift the bucket of water.
I give the stone jug a drink.
It hums softly as it drinks.
Its song flies around like a happy black *k'au*, a grackle.
The jug is no longer thirsty.
With pleasure I put my arm around its neck,
I hug him,
even though he is very naughty.
He tickles my belly and my ribs with his ear.
Perhaps he doesn't see
that I carry the bucket in my left hand,
and the rope over my shoulder.
He pleasantly spits in my hand.
He refreshes the earth where we walk.
He never stops his mischief.
Nor his tickling of my belly and ribs with his ear.
Doesn't the stone jug think by the way he makes me laugh
I might drop and break him?
He sees nothing,
he thinks nothing.
He is only devoted to making me laugh.

NAJ

Le naja' tu ye'esik u ch'ala'atel
síiskunaja'an tumen ke'el.
Ti' u xa'anil u jo'ole'
tu ch'ajch'ajáankal u yalab ki'imak óolal.
Ti' u táan u yiche'
ts'o'ok u jawal u pokpokxiik' u páakat ku je'elsikubaj tu [páakab
   che'il kisneb.
¿Ba'ax k'iin ka wixa'ab u pak'il tumen áak'ab?
Ts'o'ok u káajal u t'inik yo' kabil u xiich'e'.
Ichile'
juntúul amej u tsolmaj u tikin xiik' xk'uulucho'ob.
Máaso'obe'
tu jáalchi'itiko'ob u jíilibil u bek'ech suumil ch'e'eneknakil.
Jáalmooye' tu tsi'iktik u k'a'asaj.
Ba'ale' leili',
kex beyo' leili' u machmaj u k'ab yéetel koot
tu báaxal pilinsuut,
tu k'íilkabtik u lu'umel.

THE HOUSE

The house shows its ribs
soaked by the cold.
From its hair of thatch
it enjoys bits of happiness.
In its face
the flutter of its gaze has ceased
in the worried frames of its windows.
When did the night piss on its walls?
It shows us its veins.
Inside
a spider has gathered the dry wings of cockroaches.
The crickets
shred the threads of silence.
There are crumbs of memories in each corner.
But like this,
even like this
the house takes the walls by the hand
and plays a ronda,
sweating dust.

TÁAN U YOK'OL K'ÓOBEN

K'óobene' tu tsikbaltikten u kuxtal.
Táan u jat'ik in wich yéetel u múuc'ik',
Tu ye'esikten u teejlil u tuunchil,
bey xan u yeellil u yich,
ku ye'esikten u ta'anil tu kíimil,
bey xan u k'áak'il ma' t'aabal tu beel.
Ku jopken yéetel u muk'yaj.
Mix ba'al ku páajtal in wa'alik.
Kin ts'áik majni ti' leti' in wich
ka páajchak u yok'ol.

THE HEARTH WEEPS

The fireplace tells me its story.
Its breath slaps my face.
It shows me its wounds,
its scorched face,
dying ashes,
the deformity of its flames.

Ardent in its anguish,
silently,
my eyes shed tears.

MINA'ANECH TI' K'ÍIWIK

Bey binikech u náak'al chamal.
U huuts'ile' óoli' ku chukik a paach.
Ku luk'ikech bej.
Ku ta'akikech náach.
Je' k'íiwiko':
ti' ku wo'och' máako'obi';
leti'obe' tuunicho'ob ku balk'aláankilo'ob;
táan u yach'iko'ob in pixaan.
Je' k'íiwiko':
tu pilinsut u sáasilil u yich;
táan u kaxantikech.
Ma' tu yu'ubik u ki' péechak' a wook ti' u yoot'el,
tumen ts'o'ok a bin.

THE PLAZA WITHOUT YOU

You disappeared the way a cigarette burns down.
The smoke still lingers.
The road swallows you.
The distance hides you.
Out there on the plaza:
the people gather;
they are tumbling stones;
crushing my soul.
The eyes of the plaza scan back and forth
seeking you.
It cannot feel your soft tread on its skin,
because you are gone.

IN K'AABA'

In k'aaba'e',
tikín oot'el,
chi'il chi' u chi'ichi'al,
u cha'acha'al tumen u ts'a'ay máako'ob.
Ts'o'ok in pitik u nook'il in k'aaba'
je' bix u pots'ikubal kaan tu xla' sóol.
¿Báanten ma' táan u ya'ala'al xkáakbach ti' uj?
Leti'e' suuk u xíinbal bul áak'ab,
suuk u bulik u wíinklil,
suuk u balik u su'utal,
suk u t'ubkubaj ich eek'joch'e'enil tumen ts'o'ok
u p'ektik u sáasil.
Tumen leti'e' sak ki'ichpan xba'aba'al.
In k'aba'e'
cha' ta'aka'an ti' paalal.
In k'aba'e'
tatak'cha'ata'an tumen p'eek.
Bejla'e' mina'an in k'aaba'.
Tene' aluxen táan in so'oso'ok't'ik u tso'otsel u pool yaamaj.

MY NAME

My name,
a stuffed hide,
bitten by one mouth then another,
chewed by the fangs of the people.
I have stripped off the garment of my name
like a serpent sheds its skin.
Why don't you call the moon a whore?
She's used to walking the streets at night,
used to laying down her body,
used to concealing her shame,
used to disappearing in the darkness
because she detests her clarity.
Because she is a beautiful white pest.
My name
is the chewing gum forbidden to children.
My name
has been trampled by disgust.
Now I have no name.
I am the *aluxe* that tousles love's hair.

The *aluxe* is a Maya jungle elf known for its practical jokes.

IN YUUM

In yuum,
la'ik,
ame' táan u jit'ik u k'aan ta jo'ol.
¿Máax paal joch u xik'naal ch'íich'o'ob tu táan a jo'olal?
A ta'akmabaj ka ta jaantaj u ch'ujkil piits'.
La'ik bix pa'apa'ak'ki ta me'ex.
Tak a moojtun ta machaj.
¿Ma' wáaj taak a wenel?
Tin wilik tu paach a wich bóoch'en bóoch' yóok'ol a paakat.
In yuum,
a'al ti' in na' ka u much p'o' a pool,
a táan jo'olal,
bey xan a me'ex yéetel a moojtun.
Xeen much wenel,
tu yo'olal u je'elsikubaj u paach a wich,
ka jóok'ok xíinxinbal a paakat
je' bix jo'oljakile'.

FATHER

Father, look,
a spider has woven its hammock in your hair.
What little child has sketched the flight of birds on your forehead?
You've been secretly eating cotton candy.
Look how you've stained your mustache,
even your eyebrows.
Don't you want to sleep?
A shadow has fallen across your gaze.
Father,
tell Mommy to wash your hair,
your face,
your mustache and eyebrows.
Go to sleep,
rest your drooping eyelids,
so that you can wake refreshed
like yesterday.

CHAAMBEL K'AAY

Teche' ma' ta manaj u yúunbal xáakil u wenel a paalal.
A k'abo'ob yúunt utl'al u wenelo'ob tak'akbalo'ob ta tseem,
Mi tumen a woojel chichan paalal
mina'an u xikino'ob utia'al u yu'ubiko'ob u k'aay chi';
u chan muunmun xikino'ob
chen u ki' ki' chaambel k'aay u puksi'ik'al u na' ku yu'ubiko'ob.

GENTLE FOLKSONG

You did not buy a cradle for your children.
Your embrace lulled them to sleep cuddled to your chest.
Perhaps because you know babies
are deaf to the songs of the mouth;
their tiny, fragile ears
only hear the soft song of the mother's heart.

A NA'

A na'e' ki'imakchaj u yóol.
Ichil u jach taamil u yich
p'óoch u yaamaj.
x-Aalansaj tu ya'alaj ti' leti' ko'olel ken u síis
le ka tu paktaj ch'uyukbalech tu pak'xuuxil u chun u nak' a na'.
A na'e' ki'imakchaj u yóol.
Ti' u jach popok'look u ts'íibol pepekxik'naj u ch'e'eneknakil.
Leti'e' bin jel ka'a síijik kun síijikech.

YOUR MOTHER

You made your mother happy.
From the very depth of her eyes
love was hatched.
The midwife told her that you would be a girl
when she saw you moving inside your mother.
It made your mother happy.
In the bubbling of her grief
she broke her silence.

She was born again by your birth.

JE' BIX CHÚUK

Ja'alibe' ka síijech,
box neek' ich chan ch'uupal.
Seen boox je' bix u tóok chúuk a yuum,
je'ex u paach u kuum a na',
je'ex u paach u xaamach.
Je' bix u neek' u yich ch'e'en táan u ju'ulul tumen éek'joch'e'enil.

LIKE CHARCOAL

And then you were born,
a little girl with very black eyes.
As black as the charcoal your father makes.
Like your mother's kettle,
like the bottom side of the tortilla grill,
like the well's water when the darkness strikes it.

A YÁAX TUUP

Tumen chan ch'up síijikech,
a na'e' tu jíiltaj jun t'i'in u bek'ech súumil u puksi'ik'al
ka tu julaj ta xikin a yáax tuupintej.

YOUR FIRST EARRING

Because you were born a girl
your mother pulled a thread from her heart
and with it threaded your ear with your first earring.

YAAN A BIN XOOK

Le tuun le síiniko'ob ka'ach tu che'ejo'ob,
tu k'aayo'ob, tu yóok'oto'ob, táan xan u báaxal
u machmaj u k'abo'ob, léek u yok'olo'ob. Ko'olel
síisa'abil, leti'e kun jóoychokoja'atiko'ob wa ku
manak'ta'alo'ob ich yáalanaj.

Teche' yaan a bin xook.
Ma tun p'áatakech polwech.
Yan a táats'máansik u páakabil u najil a tuukul
yo'olal a wokoj ta wotoch
ma' táan a k'opik joolnaj.
Le ken a paktabaj tu yich a láak'
bin a wil ti' a maatsab,
box jul ch'iikil tu puksi'ik'al lu'um,
ku taal u yéemel a juntats' óol
ti' xan ku bin u na'akal u nojil a ch'i'ibal.
Teche' yaan a bin tu najil xook
ti' tuun u lóoch' u k'ab a na'at
bin a chuk u póojol u chun u nak' u ko'olelil a ch'i'ibal.
Ti' u tuunkuy
bin a na'ana'ajo'ot u wo'oj ts'íib mamaiki lu'um,
síis yéetel k'iin.
U nukuch yich a cha'an óolal
bin u cha'ant u yiim saatal u yóol
u ts'o'okol u wekik kuxtal yóok'ol kaab.
Teeche' yaan a bin tu najil xook
ba'ale' yan a suut ta taanaj,
ta yaalanaj,
ka bon yéetel k'uxub u chun u nak' ka',
ka u léets' a sak piik u yaak' sabak,
ka u p'ul yéetel u yik' a sak óol p'ulu'us k'áak',
ka u ch'op a wich u k'ak'al yaal u k'ab buuts',

190

YOU WILL GO TO SCHOOL

And the ants that laugh, sing,
dance and play began to cry.
A woman had been born
who would throw hot water on them
when they appeared in the kitchen.

You will go to school.
You will not be empty headed.
You will cross over the threshold of your memory
until you have entered your own house
without knocking on the door.
 And you will contemplate your reflection
to discover that from your eyelashes,
nocturnal arrows pin the earth to your heart,
reducing your simplicity
and lifting up the grandeur of your lineage.
You will go to school
and in the hollow of your hands your understanding
will drain from the womb of your race.
With your heel
you will decipher the hieroglyphics
written by dust, the sun, and wetness.
Your eyes are wide with admiration
they will contemplate your sagging breasts
after having spilled life over the earth.
You will go to school
but you will return to your house,
to your kitchen,
to paint the womb of the metate with spices
from the tongue of your underskirt's smudge,
to inflate with your lungs the bellows
that scrapes your eyes with thin fingers of smoke,

ka a xok ti' u paach a xáamach u p'ilis k'áak',
ka a xok ti' u tóoch' k'áak' u waak'.
Yaan a suut ta yaalanaj
tumen wa'ala'an u pa'atech u k'áanche'il tu'ux ka nak'ach waaj,
tumen k'óoben u ta'akmaj jump'éel néen tu chuun u nak'.
Jump'éel neen tu'ux ts'aalal a pixan.
Jump'éel néen ku yawat páaytikech
yéetel u juum u t'aan u léets' jul.

to read the sparks beneath the comal.
to read the crackle of the fire,
you will return to your kitchen
because your stool waits for you.
Because the hearth keeps a mirror in its entrails.
A mirror that is stamped with your soul's discoveries.
A mirror that you invoke
with the voice of your brilliance.

Both *metate* and *comal* are words with a Nahuatl etymology. Both refer to cooking implements common across indigenous Mexican cuisine. The metate is a stone mortar and pestle, and the comal is a flat griddle for cooking tortillas.

XOOCH'

Ts'o'ok u k'uchul xooch'.
Tu mot'ubal yo' koot,
T'uubul tu tuukul.
Máax ken u tomojchi'it
wa mix máak ku k'iin ti' le kaaja'.
U xla' báakel máako'obe' chen ka máanako'ob.
Uje' tu bonik u muknalilo'ob ch'een k'aax
ts'o'ok u káajal u lu'uk'ul tumen loobil.
Xooch'e'
tu xuuxubtik u k'aayil kuxtal.
Tumen ma' u k'aat u k'ay u kíimil.

THE OWL

The owl arrives.
It crouches on the wall.
Meditating.
Whose death should it announce
If no one lives in this village?
The fossils of the people have never been moved.
The moon paints the graves of the overgrown cemetery.
The owl
calls out a song to life.
Refusing to foretell its own death.

WOLIS T'AAN

Ch'e'ene' ma' uts tu t'aan a pulik tuunich ti'i'.
Ka ch'amik u ch'e'eneknakil.
Júumpuli' ma' uts tu t'aan báaxal beyo'.
Wa taak a báaxal tu yéetele'
woliskut a t'aane'
ka jalk'esti',
bin a wil bix ken u ka' a sutil ti' teech.

VOICE BALL

The well does not like that you throw stones.
It disturbs his tranquility.
This game does not please him.
If you wish to play with him,
make a ball of your voice,
throw it,
watch it come back to you.

SUUNEN

Suunen.
Ma' wáaj táan a wilik wa mina'anech tin wiknale',
áak'abe' ma' táan u booxtal.
Xaman eek'e' tu bubuláankal u ja'il yich.
Máaso'obe' sáatal u yóolo'ob.
Ik'e joch'okbal ti' lu'um tumen táan u muk'yaj.
Tak che' ts'o'ok u ka'anal u tuk'ik u k'abo'ob,
tu'ux mina'an a suut.
Suunen,
e'esabaj,
je' bix kóojolkech tin wiknalo',
ka ta ki' kapaj jun cháach ki'ichkelem chan k'íino'ob ichil
    in k'ab.

COME BACK

Come back.
You must realize that if you are not with me,
the night does not get dark.
Tears spring from the North star.
The crickets have fainted.
The wind lies down suffering on the ground.
Even the tree got tired of rustling its branches,
because you have not returned.
Come back,
show yourself,
like that first time,
when with delight you ignited in my hands a bouquet of beautiful
    little suns.

K'I'IK'I'IX K'IIN

Úuchakile'
múunyalo'ob ku tuunichil way yóok'ol lu'ume':
Uj na' tuun,
K'iin yuum tuun.
Jach úuchakil.
Le ka'ach múunyalo'ob ma' u yoojelo'ob ba'ax nonojbai',
le ka'ach ma' pok'en síis uj,
le ka'ach ma' yanak u k'i'ixel k'iin.

SUN WITH SPINES

At one time
the clouds were stones here on earth:
Mother stone the moon,
Father stone the sun.
Long ago
when the clouds did not know their own splendor
the moon was not cold,
nor had the sun grown spines.

ACKNOWLEDGEMENTS

The editors would like to thank the editors of the following magazines and books, where versions of some of the translations in this volume have previously appeared.

Víctor Terán's poems have appeared in *The Spines of Love* (Restless Books, 2014), *Poems/Diidxado'* (Poetry Translation Centre, 2010), *Agenda, Hayden's Ferry Review, Oxford Magazine, Poetry,* and *World Literature Today.*

Juan Gregorio Regino's poems have appeared in *Reversible Monuments: Contemporary Mexican Poetry* (Copper Canyon Press), and *María Sabina Selections* (University of California Press).

Mikeas Sánchez' poems have appeared in *Bengal Lights, The Bitter Oleander, The Drunken Boat,* and *World Literature Today.*

Juan Hernández poems have appeared in *World Literature Today.*

Briceida Cuevas Cob's poems have appeared in *The Dirty Goat* and *World Literature Today.*

TRANSLATORS

Adam W. Coon is a PhD candidate in Iberian and Latin American languages and cultures at the University of Texas at Austin. He has extensively researched present-day Nahuatl literary production throughout Mexico. His current project is entitled *Iajki Estados Onidos: The Articulation of Nahua Identities in Migration in Contemporary Nahua Literature, 1985–2012*. His translations of Juan Hernández' poems have appeared in *World Literature Today*.

Jonathan Harrington lives in an 18ᵗʰ century hacienda that he restored himself in rural Yucatán, Mexico, where he writes and translates poetry. A graduate of the University of Iowa Writers' Workshop, he has published four chapbooks: *The Traffic of Our Lives* (winner of the Ledge Press Poetry Chapbook Award) *Handcuffed to the Jukebox, Aqui/Here* (bilingual), and *Yesterday, A Long Time Ago*. His translations of Mayan poetry have appeared in *World Literature Today* and *International Poetry Review*, among others. His book length translation of the Mayan poet Feliciano Sánchez Chan (*Seven Dreams*) appeared in 2014 from New Native Press. In addition to poetry, he has edited an anthology of short stories, authored a collection of essays, and has published five novels. His poems have been translated into Spanish, French, and Arabic.

Born on December 11, 1931, **Jerome Rothenberg** was raised in New York City and graduated from the City College of New York in 1952 with a BA in English. He went on to the University of Michigan and Columbia University. Rothenberg began his literary career in the late 1950s working primarily as a translator; he is responsible for the first English appearances of Paul Celan and Günter Grass. Rothenberg has published over seventy books and pamphlets of poetry. He has translated an enormous amount of world literature, including Pablo Picasso and Vítezslav Nezval. Rothenberg is best known for his work in ethnopoetics, a term he coined, involving the synthesis of poetry, linguistics, anthropology, and ethnology. Through it he sought to both perpetuate fading oral and written literary legacies of the world and render them relevant and necessary to modern literature. His numerous awards and honors include grants from the Guggenheim Foundation and the National Endowment for the Arts; two PEN Oakland Josephine Miles Literary Awards; two PEN Center USA Translation Awards; and the San Diego Public Library's Local Author Lifetime Achievement Award. In 1997 he received a Doctorate of Letters from the State University of New York and was elected to the World Academy of Poetry in 2001.

Raised in Mexico City, poet, translator, and filmmaker **David Shook** studied endangered languages in Oklahoma and poetry at Oxford University before settling in Los Angeles, where he serves as Founding Editor of Phoneme Media. He spent the summer of 2007 living with his wife in a Guerrero Nahuatl-speaking home in the village of San Agustín Oapan, in Guerrero, Mexico. His translations from the Isthmus Zapotec, Nahuatl, and Zoque have appeared in publications including *Bitter Oleander, PN Review, Poetry,* and *World Literature Today.* His translation of Víctor Terán's *The Spines of Love* was published by Restless Books in 2014. His translations of poems by Terán and Mikeas Sánchez have been nominated for the Pushcart Prize. His own poetry has been longlisted for the International Dylan Thomas Prize.

Clare Sullivan is Associate Professor of Spanish at the University of Louisville and Director of their Graduate Certificate in Translation. She has published translations of Argentine writer Alicia Kozameh's *259 Leaps, the Last Immortal* and Mexican Cecilia Urbina's *A Tuesday Like Today* with Wings Press. She received an NEA Translation Grant in 2010 to work with the poetry of

Natalia Toledo. Her translation of Toledo's *The Black Flower and Other Zapotec Poems* will be published by Phoneme Media in 2015.

Jacob Surpin is a writer and editor living in Los Angeles. He is the Blog Editor and a Fiction Editor for the *Los Angeles Review of Books*, and the Production Coordinator and Assistant Editor for Unnamed Press. He is originally from Brooklyn, New York.

Eliot Weinberger is an essayist, political commentator, translator, and editor. His books of avant-gardist literary essays include *Karmic Traces*, *An Elemental Thing* (named by the *Village Voice* as one of the "20 Best Books of the Year") and, most recently, *Oranges & Peanuts for Sale*. His political articles are collected in *What I Heard About Iraq*—called by the *Guardian* the one antiwar "classic" of the Iraq war—and *What Happened Here: Bush Chronicles*. The author of a study of Chinese poetry translation, *19 Ways of Looking at Wang Wei*, he is the translator of the poetry of Bei Dao, and the editor of *The New Directions Anthology of Classical Chinese Poetry* and the *Calligrams* series published by NYRB Classics. His other anthologies include *World Beat: International Poetry Now from New Directions* and *American Poetry Since 1950: Innovators & Outsiders*. Among his translations of Latin American poetry and prose are the *Collected Poems 1957–1987 of Octavio Paz*, Vicente Huidbro's *Altazor*, and Jorge Luis Borges' *Selected Non-Fictions*, which received the National Book Critics Circle award for criticism. He was born in New York City, where he still lives. His work has been translated into thirty languages.

Educators interested in using *Like a New Sun* in the classroom can download a free study guide and access other teaching resources at:

www.phonememedia.org/studyguide